THE BIGGEST CHALLENGE

'THE EARTH IS DYING'

LIFE, WHAT ON EARTH IS IT ALL ABOUT?

STEP ONE | ASKING QUESTIONS

DR RAY HALL

The Cunningham Press

First published in Great Britain in 2020 by The Cunningham Press

Picture Credits

All images from the author's personal collection apart from the following:
Sir David Attenborough by World Bank Photo Collection is licensed under CC BY-NC-ND 2.0
Grooming Tiger by Koshyk is licensed under CC BY 2.0
Sir David Attenborough by World Bank Photo Collection is licensed under CC BY-NC-ND 2.0
Greta Thunberg by World Economic Forum is licensed under CC BY-NC-SA 2.0
Cliff Birds by Ray Muzyka is licensed under CC BY-NC-SA 2.0
John Hancock Center by Matthew Black is licensed under CC BY-SA 2.0
Prism by iwannt is licensed under CC BY 2.0.

ISBN: 978-1-5272-7667-3

10 9 8 7 6 5 4 3 2 1

A CIP catalogue record for this book is available from the British Library.

WITH THANKSGIVING

These pages have been written with a deep thanksgiving for:

Jessie and Norman as my amazing mum and dad

My brilliantly loving wife, Jenny

My terrific daughters, Becs and Claire

Claire's highly capable husband, Sam, and their new-born babe, Ella Sophia

As well as Poppy, their huggable doggie

And for the many people and the many places

I will highlight as we journey forward

Step by Step

They have also been written because of an ever-deeper appreciation for:

Our amazing Earth and its host cosmos

As well as an 'even more' that indwells the whole of life

Imagine a young man, sitting on a surfboard

He is looking out to sea that represents a lifetime ahead

He realises what is out there

It is a dying Earth

He asks fundamental questions about his life

About all our lives and

About life itself

A journey of a lifetime followed

Some 50 years later, these pages are the outcome

CONTENTS

Images 9

Heading One: INTRODUCTION 13

Heading Two: THE VIEWS OF OTHERS 19

Heading Three: SCENE SETTING 31

Heading Four: A BOY BECAME A MAN 55

Heading Five: BELONGING AND CONTEXT 79

Heading Six: A DESIGN BRIEF AND CLOTHING 113

Heading Seven: DIAGRAMS 137

Heading Eight: PING PONG BALLS 165

Heading Nine: ALREADY THERE 181

Heading Ten: ALREADY HAPPENING 195

A SUMMARY OF QUESTIONS RAISED 218

IMAGES

Heading One: INTRODUCTION

1: Ray and Jenny by the River Thames 13

Heading Two: THE VIEWS OF OTHERS

2: *Sunday Times Magazine* cover 26.02.1989 17

3: An informed insight 19

4: Even our diets have to change 19

5: My spiral diagrams 28

Heading Three: SCENE SETTING

6: When I look back 31

7: Me in short trousers 35

8: A slightly older Ray 37

9: Millions of trees are being planted 44

10: Two more timely encouragements 45

11a & b: And two more 47 & 48

Heading Four: A BOY BECAME A MAN

12: Ray and Jenny by the River Thames 55

13: Members of the Co-op in Darlington 61

14: A green energy generating inhabited bridge 69

15: My mum with Rita, Becs and Claire 74

Heading Five: BELONGING AND CONTEXT

16: A cliff edge 79

17: An early brochure sheet 85

18: My current logo 86

19: An insulating porch for two elderly ladies 97

20: A New Eco Crystal Palace 98

Heading Six: A DESIGN BRIEF AND CLOTHING

21: More than just a porch 113

Heading Seven: DIAGRAMS

22: Emerging theory diagrams 137

23: Three separate circles overlapping as one 139

24: Three separate circles 140

25: Two circles overlapping 141

26: Two-as-one relating to a third 141

27: Three circles overlapping 141

28: Three circles overlapping as one 142

29: A sequence of circle diagrams 143

30: Ecological dimensions in life 144

31: I am holding my nephew, Cristian 153

32: Ella Sophia now in my arms 154

Heading Eight: PING PONG BALLS

33: Three ping pong balls, with all touching 165

34: Six ping pong balls around one in 2-D 168

35: Twelve ping pong balls around one in 3-D 170

36: Triangulation in a stool 171

37: A cross-braced office building 173

Heading Nine: ALREADY THERE

38: Light passing through a prism 181

Heading Ten: ALREADY HAPPENING

39: A breakdown diagram 195

40: *A Blueprint for Survival* 198

41: Headline in the *Observer* & Critic's Choice 202

42: My breakdown diagram 207

Heading One

INTRODUCTION

Image 1:

I thought it might be helpful if you saw what I look like. I am here with Jenny.

Do note the setting of a bridge and a river

Its relevancy will become clear as we journey forward

When studying to be an Architect in the early 1970s, I realised that:

a. The Earth and all of life has within it a design language;

b. It is a language that speaks;

c. It is a design language that frames a central desire in all our lives, which is to belong. I also realised that;

d. Our home planet is, tragically, in such trouble that it is dying.

As the last insight registered in 1972, tears flowed, as they have done since as a further realisation dawned. It is that the deeply tragic issues of climate change and extinctions point to something much more. I, therefore, wanted to understand a bigger context and studied Planning. It was then that I also realised what is, perhaps, obvious and easily overlooked. It was that the way we see the world affects how we live.

As a result, I began to seek out a world view that:

a. Makes sense of the existence of a design language in life, of belonging and also of death; and one that;

b. Points to how I and we could respond, both in theory and in practice.

These pages are the outcome and are a form of summary journal. For, they host a journey of a lifetime. It is a journey of personal insights, with ideas that are based on observing everyday life. None is in isolation, for each has applications in practice. Because of the nature of my life's work, visual images are frequent and as part of what is akin to a scrapbook.

I see each insight and image as a contribution to a debate that must involve us all. For, we human beings are facing THE BIGGEST CHALLENGE ever. It is that our planetary home is in trouble, with many now beginning to say that it is dying.

The implications of that prospect are vast and the subject areas they generate are as huge as they are detailed. I have, therefore, set out my own response as a series of 'Steps'. They start with an ever-enlarging number of questions. Each question then leads to an ever deeper understanding of our context. From there what are, for me, very practical answers then follow. By being open with you and setting out my own questions, with answers following, my goal is that each can then be tested, accepted, dismissed, added to or varied.

When tabling them, I am also inviting others to set out their response to our shared predicament and to do so for testing. My suggestion then is that our shared goal must be a viable way of not only understanding life. It must also be one that works in practice, whilst there is time.

As you start to turn these pages, you may find yourself identifying with some aspects of my own journey of a lifetime. You may then want to add your own. You may also not identify with any. If that is the case, do set out your own insights and, from there, your own reasons why. If you have not already done so, you may even be able to set out the Steps in your journey of a lifetime. If that happens, I would be pleased. For, I have come to one core conclusion on my own journey. It is that we all need each other, when facing what is ahead.

Aspects of my life may surprise you, as may some of my conclusions so far. Whatever your response, my desire is 100% that you will feel able to set out your own insights. For, my trust is that we can all learn from each other and do so as part of what could then become THE BIG DEBATE as, together, we seek solutions to the predicament before us.

It is a debate that must lead to viable answers. If you would like to send in your responses as part of such a debate, the email address is...

ABIGDEBATE@gmail.com

It is in that context that THE BIGGEST CHALLENGE now facing our global community is not just of a dying Earth. It goes even further than that and is:

LIFE, WHAT ON EARTH IS IT ALL ABOUT?

And especially if:

LIFE IS IN THE CONTEXT OF DEATH.

I will start my contribution to THE BIG DEBATE with a glimpse of the views of others, who are noting what is happening to our Earth, including a *Sunday Times* headline from 1989.

Image 2: *Sunday Times* of February 26th, 1989. I will come back to it

Heading Two

THE VIEWS OF OTHERS

'Collapse of civilisation is on the horizon'

Sir David Attenborough

The TV naturalist used an address at the UN climate change summit in Katowice, Poland, to tell delegates from 200 nations: 'The people have spoken out. They want you, the decision makers, to act now.' Attenborough said the world's warming climate was 'a manmade disaster' and the biggest threat to humanity 'in thousands of years'.

'Act now – or face the collapse of civilisation'

Attenborough's climate change warning

» Time is running out, naturalist tells United Nations climate talks

» Trump 'out on a limb' with withdrawal from Paris accord

» UN Secretary-Genera[l] warns it 'is already a matter of life and death'

Go mostly vegetarian to save the world, UN urges

Massive reduction in meat consumption is needed to protect habitats, report into biodiversity finds

By **Emma Gatten**
ENVIRONMENT EDITOR
and **Olivia Rudgard** *in San Francisco*

MOVING to mostly vegetarian diets will be crucial to save the natural world, the United Nations has warned.

Plant and animal species are being lost at unprecedented rates because of human activity, according to a report that says none of 20 biodiversity goals set 10 years ago have been achieved.

Cutting meat consumption would reduce the destruction of forests and other lands, as well as cutting greenhouse gas emissions that contribute to climate change.

In its five-year report on the Aichi biodiversity targets in 2015, the UN merely advocated a reduction in meat consumption but it has now joined calls for people to embrace a mostly plant-based diet.

It comes after the World Wide Fund for Nature warned that reversing an average 68 per cent drop in global wildlife species since 1970 would only be possible if meat in diets is halved.

Of the 20 biodiversity goals, set out by the UN and agreed in 2011 by almost 200 countries, none have been fully achieved and just six were partially achieved, the fifth Global Biodiversity Outlook said. The targets included reducing the destruction of rainforests and mangroves, cutting pollution and sustainable fisheries management. Even the target of raising awareness of species loss has not been fully met.

'The warning lights are flashing... if we carry on with business as usual, we'll be out of business'

Top: Image 3: An informed insight
Below: Image 4: Even our diets have to change

In 1972, when completing my Finals written thesis, my conclusion was that our Earth is dying. As I have mentioned, tears came then, just as they have on many occasions since. They have come as the harsh reality of that expectation began to register.

As a result, my life has since been about understanding:

a. Why that prospect exists and;

b. How we can all, with me included, respond to what is the biggest challenge ever to face humanity.

My trust then is that the insights and proposals in these pages may be a helpful contribution to THE BIG DEBATE. It is one that needs to be on a scale and to a depth of detail, perhaps, never previously known throughout the history of this astonishing, as well as wonderful, planet. It is also a debate that must have outcomes that are positive for the well-being, not just of every person, but also of every living being on this our planetary home.

My own work arena for five decades has been designing and building places that, on a variety of scales, have sought to fit the lives of people. Throughout, my goal has been that people will enhance places and do so for the benefit of life here on Earth. As a result, my own way of seeing the world has been substantially through that specific means of serving others, as people and as places. That is why, in the pages that follow, you will find many analogous comparisons from that arena, as I have sought to anchor my world view theory into my work and do so in practice.

It has then been with the desire that others will feel able to do the same in their own daily lives and, hence, through the medium of their own workplace, as well as leisure-based arenas. For, it is a whole life approach that is needed, if we are to be able to respond effectively to the enormous challenge that we all now face.

Allow me now to be more specific about my work context. For, throughout my decades of serving others, my goal has been that:

a. People become more able to belong with others and do so in the place that they live, work and enjoy their leisure time. It has also been;

b. That both people and places can play their role ever more effectively in the shared global challenge that I have highlighted and;

c. It is how to enable an endangered, even dying, Earth to live for as long and as positively as possible.

That is why, when as a student, I founded and led for 34 years what became a small multidisciplinary design and property practice, based in London, called 'People and Places'. For reasons that I will explain, in 2007 that practice closed. In the years since, my focus has been shaping major development strategies through a different vehicle, 'People and Places International'. Both initiatives have been a response to my Finals' thesis conclusion.

That ongoing journey came into focus as the year AD 2000 approached. For, it was then that I realised that our global community was about to leave the last complete Millennium of 1,000 years of life here on our Earth. I also concluded that our current Third Millennium would be short-lived. As a result, I described the Second Millennium as being: 'The last complete Millennium for life here on Earth'. As we left AD 2000, humanity was, therefore, entering what was expected to be a limited period in:

'THE LAST MILLENNIUM'

As we journey forward through this and each subsequent Step, I will explore the enormous and far reaching implications of that conclusion and, from there, the predicament we now all face. I will also table my own positive, big picture as well as detailed, response. It will be when knowing that the reality of our situation is increasingly recognised around our world. As I sought my own answers to the many profound questions that awareness generated, it soon became clear that there are none that are easy. For, there are no quick fixes. A lot of work was needed in order to begin to understand, with rigorous testing following. Both were necessary before answers could be seen to have the coherence needed and, from there, with actions that had any degree of credibility.

As a result, it soon became evident that time was needed to understand our context and hence the reason why for the core issue I had to face. That context included a flow of history that has led us all to a form of precipice. That bigger and long-term context was, therefore, needed and urgently so. It was also when knowing that rushing to ill-considered solutions could potentially make our situation even more precarious. For, they could accelerate the arrival of life's end here on Earth. That is why I found myself asking many fundamental questions, with each leading to answers. You will learn of quite a number of those questions in this first Step. For, my goal is to set a context for what then follows in future Steps, with answers unfolding.

The direction that journey takes may come as a surprise. For, it focuses on, what was for me, an unexpected way of seeking answers that could lead to outcomes that work in practice. That way forward was, crucially, evidence based.

I have been aware of our global predicament for almost fifty years. During that time, my understanding of my own future has been based on its prospect. For many, when knowing of what lies ahead, the future must now seem, at minimum, uncertain, other than having to somehow cope with the notion of an end. Even when feeling such uncertainty, our lives in the present exist and life is still rooted in our past. That is why it became of crucial importance that I understood what is happening now, not just in the context of human history, but also in the history of life itself.

A way forward had, therefore, to be about how our relatively recent era fits in our Earth's distant past. For, now is, in a sense, an extension of our past. Our shared future here on Earth is then the same. It is rooted in our shared past. As each Step unfolds, my own core answers are set in that context, as I explore in increasing depth an ever bigger past, present and future picture. I will do so always with applications in our own era today. That onward journey then moves toward a climax. It is with a way forward of substance that is focused on that future, set in the context of history.

It is a way forward that is then offered for consideration, as well as debate, whilst there is time.

Throughout the journey of my own lifetime, there was the constant need to learn and then for rigorous testing of the conclusions I began to reach. As a result, I deliberately placed myself in contexts where I could engage with others, who could then test what I was thinking. As part of that ongoing process, in my late 60s, I enrolled in a programme toward a Professional Doctorate. Its focus was defining and then applying theories about life in specialist arenas, my own being designing places. Crucially, a goal was to test outcomes in day-to-day practice. That process then fed into this written journey here.

I am now 72. I have had a lot of time to define and outwork theory into practice. Because my point of reference has been the whole of life, you will see that I have deliberately seen dimensions of my own personal life as a resource. As a result, I have, in a sense, placed my life on the line by using examples of theory learned during my ascending years. That includes my work as a designer of places. It is so that you can then assess the credibility of the insights gained and conclusions reached so far.

As I trust will become evident, I have sought to do so in as focused and as broad a context as was possible. My desire is that we will also feel able to do the same, with a two way, shared and rigorous debate then being able to follow.

By the way, you do not have to be a university don or even a student to be able to enter such a debate. Every one of us has something of value to contribute, no matter our background, age and context. For, such must be an all-embracing debate, with everyone involved being vital. That is because the outcome will affect us all. It is in that context that one early conclusion on my own journey was specific. It was that:

EVERYBODY IS DIFFERENT AND EVERYBODY IS SPECIAL

AND WE ALL NEED EACH OTHER

I will then add two more words. They are:

ESPECIALLY NOW.

That is because the time remaining here on Earth may now be very limited and, perhaps, only a matter of decades. Even if we are privileged to have more time, the end will still come for me and for you. It would also seem to be coming for our planetary home, our precious, life-enabling Earth.

It is now some 50 years since my student days. Throughout those decades, the realisation that came when writing my Finals' thesis has become increasingly real and disturbingly so. Do, therefore, be ready to learn about more tears as we journey forward. It may even be that you will feel some rise too.

My own will not, however, only be as a result of the pain of anticipated loss. There will also be tears wrought by joy. That is because to be alive is an amazing privilege. To be alive on an Earth as fabulous as this one is then beyond amazing. To be able to call it 'home' is a privilege that is even beyond measure. As we journey forward, it is in the context of such joy in the midst of tears that I trust we will be able to enter into realms that I will try to describe. It will be when knowing that my words will, inevitably, be inadequate.

As a result, do get ready. There is quite a journey ahead. It is one of tears caused by pain as well as joy. It is also one that seeks to reconcile what I see as being core contradictions in life. For, life is indeed in the context of death. At the same time, a heartbeat in life is evident in belonging.

But, there is more. For, early in my own journey, I concluded that belonging is rooted in love. It is a desire to love and be loved that indwells and motivates people. It is a belonging rooted in love that, inevitably, manifests itself when we live in places. That principle, I am sure, applies to everyone, no matter who or where we are around our world. It was when realising its importance, that I made a commitment concerning my future work life. It was to enable such a sense of belonging, using emerging design skills. It was to do so, when loving and serving others as people and as places.

Clearly, the contrast is stark between belonging by people in a place and an end to sustainable life here on Earth. For, one destroys the other. That further realisation led to a lifetime seeking a positive answer to the question that is the subtitle here, which I amplified to become. It is:

IF LIFE IS IN THE CONTEXT OF DEATH,

WHAT ON EARTH IS LIFE ALL ABOUT?

The issue of death is not one that is distant for me. Being the age I am, it could come in the relatively near future. My dad died when he was 62 and my mum at an age similar to mine. My sister also died some while ago. I am, as a result, the last remaining member of my immediate blood family, with universal evidence that confirms that my end will also come. Clearly, I am far from being alone when knowing that death is on its way.

To state the obvious, when it happens, I will not be able to think, speak, remember or write. That prospect has been an added incentive when preparing these many pages. For, my trust is that the insights shared will be of help to you and to others. This is especially when knowing that each insight has informed, motivated and framed very practical outcomes in the many design projects that I – and the teams working with me – have carried out. You will see some of those projects, which range from a draught-excluding porch to a series of strategies that could transform half of London into a green energy powerhouse.

The thinking that led to each also enabled me to table two proposals for democratically based management strategies. One would enable the UK to be governed far more effectively as we prepare for what is to come. Another relates to a restructuring of the United Nations in order to help enable our Earth to live for as long as is possible.

These pages really do, therefore, tell of a lifetime's journey shaping theory and applying it in practice. There has been a lot of failure along the way. It has also been a journey that continues to be engrained in the lives of many people, as well as many places. Each is then part of the life we all share. As a result, the pages that now follow also host newspaper headlines and articles that tell of the context in which we all live. There are then photographs as glimpses, not only into my daily life, but also the life we all share. All are part of what I trust is the thoughtful scrapbook that is my goal, albeit one that is framed by an issue that is deadly serious.

As a detail, these pages were completed in the summer of 2020, with quite a long period of preparation. My inclusion, in Image 2, of a *Sunday Times Magazine* cover from 1989 is an indication. You could, therefore, add other newspaper headlines, as events locally and globally will have moved on by the time you read these paragraphs.

As I trust you will appreciate, the format I have adopted has been deliberate. For, my goal is that we all feel able to make our lives accessible, so that we can learn from each other and then act together in as purposeful a way as possible. It is to do so when adding a phrase that I have already used. It is, 'whilst there is time'.

As a result, my key message is that we all have a role to play in seeking, gaining and living answers to enormous questions. This is especially when knowing that the context is as deadly as it is serious, even climactic. We may all then be able to help our Earth to, not only live for as long as possible, but also do so in a way that is potentially very meaningful indeed. Life lived meaningfully is, as a result, a two-as-one with each informing the other.

When knowing that my themes will be personal as well as global, allow me now to say a little more about me.

As you have seen from my first page of dedications, I am very grateful to be married to Jenny. Our home, for almost all of our adult lives, was in Lewisham in southeast London. We now live in Witney, near Oxford. We are both very grateful to be the parents of two grown-up daughters, a very able son-in-law and a precious, recently born granddaughter. A doggie called Poppy then completes the picture of our growing family. Together, we all belong together as one.

During my seven decades of life, I have been privileged to count many people as dear friends, with whom I also belong. As we journey forward, you will meet some of those, always special, people. I have also come to some stark conclusions. They included one as we approached AD 2000. I summarised it as the challenge we all face and did so in one phrase. It was:

THE LAST MILLENNIUM

The newspaper cuttings at the beginning of this heading point to its implications. Before I explore those implications more fully, allow me to reaffirm that my response is fundamentally positive to the deadly predicament before us all. That is not because I think the problem is not real. Far from it. Nor is it because I think the issues we face are easily resolved. For, as you have seen, my view is the opposite. My positivity is because, I have, since my student days, sought to:

a. Face the many implications of an end to viable life here on Earth, as well as;

b. Face, what I would suggest is, the prospect that there is nowhere else in our cosmos where we could all go. It was to then;

c. Try, in my own limited way, to understand what is happening and why by asking huge questions and then exploring answers that have informed a multitude of decisions over many decades, with;

d. Each being relevant to my private, as well as my work, life, set in the context of a growing understanding of the reason why for the whole of life.

Having suggested that we all need to do the same, I must now emphasise something I have already mentioned. It is that I am very aware that I have failed. Even when I have to some degree succeeded, I have also failed. I suspect we are all in that same 'boat'. I will say more on both as we journey forward.

So that you are aware, I considered adding a question mark after 'THE LAST MILLENNIUM'. Sadly, I concluded that the answer is now becoming too self-evident. A possible question, therefore, became the statement that I have made. Many people are now coming to a similar conclusion, just as others are also doubting that view. Some are not saying what they think. I can understand such hesitancy, because what is coming toward us is almost too frightening and overwhelming to dare even to consider. I also know from experience that, when facing it, the impact can then be profound. Everything in life is then affected.

For me, as you have seen, its harsh reality led to uncontrollable tears in my student days, just as it has in the decades since. Our shared predicament is, as a result, difficult to live with. Indeed, a big part of me would prefer what is coming not to be the case. Tragically, I would be misleading everyone if I suggested that an end was not on its way. I do not know the specific timing of that end, although some are saying it will be sooner rather than later and hence in decades and not centuries.

Many years ago, when I shared my headline question about life's reason why with a flatmate, he told me that no one can answer it. If that is the case, there are then, at least, three implications:

a. It will be impossible to discern answers to the many other questions that inevitably follow, including many that I am raising here;

b. That impossibility means that we are all heading irreversibly into a future and doing so whilst 'flying blind'. There is then one further implication. It is;

c. There are dangers ahead that, hypothetically, could have been avoided.

Despite that doubting and because the predicament we all face is so serious, I did not accept my flatmate's view and decided to keep going. Decades later, I am confident that there are answers to even these huge questions, as well as every other question that then follows. As a result, I am certain we can all table our own questions and seek our own answers. We can also then discuss and debate, with the goal of discerning a viable way forward and respond accordingly.

I will go one step further and say that my view is that a viable way forward is 'already there' waiting to be grasped. It is one that is relevant in every arena of life. Do note that I have highlighted the phrase 'already there'. For, I will come back to its meaning and implications as we journey forward. Before doing so, it is important that I explain that the journey ahead will be linear and, hence with a beginning, a middle and an end. It will also be akin to two spirals.

The first will be inward and in such a way as to embrace an increasing number of issues in ever greater depth. In the process key themes will be explored in ever greater detail. That will lead to a pivotal point of reference. An outward spiral of unpacking theory and applying it in practice then commences. As a result, practical answers will follow to the many questions raised as part of an outward journey. Those answers will then be part of my one total, spiral-in and spiral-out picture, with so much more still to be explored.

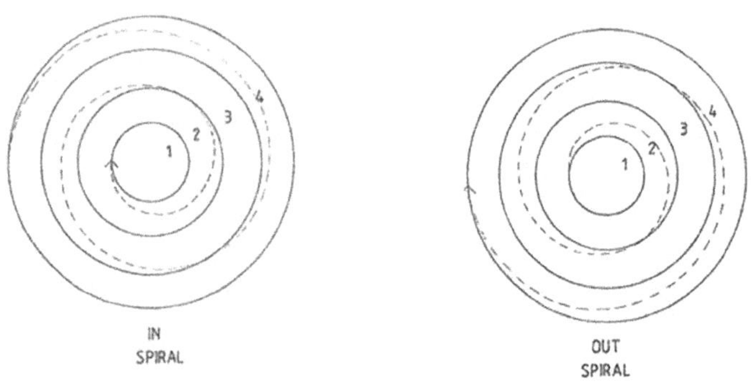

Image 5: My spiral diagrams

My trust is that spiral-in and spiral-out journeys may then be positive contributions to THE BIG DEBATE now needed in the context of THE BIGGEST CHALLENGE facing us all.

I will conclude this heading with two thoughts. The first is to highlight a diagram that tells of a journey that spirals-in and one that spirals-out. As with so many of those diagrams, I drew each when as a student studying Architecture and hence the design of places that fit the lives of people. I will explain the relevance of the concentric circles, with their numbers, later.

The second is from my schoolboy cricketing days when I enjoyed catching balls in the 'slips'. There is a special feeling when a hand is open and in the right place to catch a ball that speeds off a bat. Diving to do so was often needed. I will now add that analogy to the others I have used. For, each theme I will explore could be seen to be akin to a finger, which, when seen with other themes, becomes a hand held open and ready. That hand is then, in effect, the same shape as the ball. It is not the ball, but the only way the ball can be caught is by shaping a form of receptacle in readiness.

Relate the ball to my answer to the big question 'why?' and my hand to a context of themes that I will describe about life. My goal is then that, Step by Step, the 'hand' of our lives may be able to catch this ball. You may choose to drop it. You may also decide to hold it and throw it to someone else to hold as the game or journey we all share in life continues. Whatever your choice, being able to decide is the privilege we all share.

Heading Three

SCENE SETTING

Image 6: When I look back

Almost 50 years ago, I was young like the lad on the surfboard on the front cover

The actual me is in the middle of this amusing photograph, with untidy long hair

I was not on a surfboard, but with student friends travelling between Greek islands

We had just completed our architectural training

Michael Keniger is to the left, with hair freshly cut

He later became Professor of Architecture in Queensland University

I should have had mine trimmed as well (!)

At this point, you might understandably be asking:

'Why does this Ray Hall think he has something to contribute to a debate about life's reason why? It has already been debated in a multitude of contexts and, no doubt, over millennia.'

My answer is that I can because I think we can all contribute. For, I am a human being and, just like you, I was born. For me, it was in 1947. I then grew to become the now ageing man I am today. As anyone accumulating years will know, I have experienced a lot in life. I do not know how old you are. Nevertheless, I am sure, the same principle applies. For, you too are accumulating experiences in life.

This is also when knowing my contributions to date have not always been as helpful as they could have been.

My life focus has been, what I call, the design relationship between people and places. It has been about the many-layered environments in which we live: hence me studying Architecture. When using the terms 'people' and 'places', in the five or so decades of my working life, there has been increasing evidence of that relationship being in decline around our Earth. Despite my own positive endeavours, I am sure that I have contributed to that negative outcome. Even though my commitment has been the opposite, I have, therefore, been part of the problem. It is a fact in life that saddens me greatly.

What then adds to that tragedy is another fact. It is that I am sure I am a long way from being alone as a contributor to the predicament we all now face. Indeed, my expectation is that every generation throughout history has made their contribution. If that is the case, then we all face a challenge that is personal. It is between:

a. A heartfelt desire to make a positive contribution toward resolving the predicament we all face; whilst also;

b. Recognising that, at the same time, with me as an example, I have been contributing to the opposite. Indeed, by simply being alive, I am then still doing so. My expectation is that the same applies to you, as well.

As you will see, alongside my core question, many other related questions have been added. With each has come even more challenges. This has been, especially, when seeking a point of reference for the many personal, as well as design, decisions I knew I would have to make throughout my working life. The issue at hand is, as a result, as objectively relevant to an ever bigger yet also direct context, as it is subjectively deeply personal. It is a context that then embraces everything we all do and unavoidably affects us all.

When thinking personally, I am immensely grateful for each of the special people with whom I belong. Add to people, the many places where I have lived as well as visited. My gratitude cannot but then overflow. I am sure you will be able to say the same in relation to the many equivalent people and places in your life. From there, together we can affirm that such appreciation must also abound around our world. For, we are then glimpsing how special all of the people and all the places are, wherever we live on this our planetary home. Add to that large number of special people in special places, the many more that have lived throughout history. The shared experience of belonging is a constellation that is vast.

At the same time, I am very aware of so much pain in our individual, as well as in our shared lives. Such pain is being felt now and has been long into the past. In its midst is the harsh reality that the reason for pain can be a forerunner that leads to death. Many then describe that outcome as, 'the one certainty in life'. It would now seem that our Earth, including all the people and places dear to each one of us, is in such serious trouble that it too faces that same certainty.

When I look back from my 73rd year, I am aware that there were few predicting that outcome in my youth. There was then a small number, more as we left the Second Millennium and entered the Third, but the number is now accelerating. Am I pleased that that awareness is now growing, perhaps exponentially?

My answer is 'yes' as well as 'no'.

For, in AD 2000, my children were in their teens, with their own student days ahead and a life of aspirations. When enjoying their expectations, I became even more aware that the predicament we are all facing not only applied to me. It applied to them as well and, perhaps, even more so. The term 'everyone', therefore, acquired a dimension that went from a overview to being very deep. It then hit the core of my being and it will not go away. The same principle then applied to the word 'everywhere'. For, my children now have adult lives of their own, with belongings with many other people in many other places.

As I write, it is AD 2020, which is a number that is often associated with seeing long distances, as well as anticipating new futures. From there it is associated with what could be called, visionary thinking. Anticipating the future is certainly my goal here. As will become evident as we journey forward, my goal is to do so when also seeing long distances into the past. For, I am certain that one is fully dependent upon the other. As a result, the answer to any question rooted in 'why' inhabits that continuum.

In terms of my own past and future, I am now towards the end of my life here on planet Earth. You may be at a similar position, just as you may also be closer to the beginning of your own life. I do not know. Having said that, none of us knows exactly when the end of our lives will come. Even though my time is now more limited than ever, I still do not know the detail of my own end. I am, however, confident in some of the detail of my beginning. For, like you, I am certain that I was born in a specific place and at an equally specific point in time.

Almost certainly like you, I cannot remember the moment of my birth. For my mum, the opposite was the case. Every moment was very real, so much so that she told me that I was early by some weeks and looked like a 'skinned rabbit' when she first saw me. I am pleased to report that, despite those first appearances, I was a greatly welcomed arrival. I have since realised that not everyone can relate to such a welcome. For, not every new-born child is appreciated, which is a deep sadness that makes me even more grateful for the context of my own beginning.

As a child, I felt vulnerable. You will be able to sense that in the photograph in Image 7. For, I am the shy little boy, who stayed close to his mum's skirts.

Image 7: Me in short trousers with my mum, whose life enabled mine

I then grew up knowing that I was loved. That, in turn, led to me feel a special sense of being as one with my family in the several places where we lived. That precious awareness later became my key point of reference for so much that has since followed in my now lengthening life.

As I grew to adulthood, that sense of belonging grew. It was then that I began to agonise over the reality that my parents would inevitably die, as would all those dear to me. In my early student years, I also realised that we all face that terminal prospect. No matter who or where we are in our global community, an end applied. When completing my Finals written thesis, the further realisation then came that the same applies to the Earth on which we all depend for life.

Questions concerning that seeming contradiction between belonging and death then slowly led to answers that, in turn, informed my work. As we journey forward, you will be able to assess whether that contradiction has been resolved in theory, as well as in practice and especially in my own work arena.

As you do so, one thing is certain. Even if you are 50 years younger than me, your life span is like mine. It is limited and one day it will come to an end. It would now also seem that that is in prospect for our planetary home. It is one that is, therefore, as personal as it is global.

Allow me now to take this direction of thought another step further.

When I have asked questions about why life is like this, I have also asked why it is that each life has a beginning, with always the certainty of an end. As a result, life is specific, with a finite context. I then concluded that any answers had to be a practical response to that defined constraint. The importance of being practical was then further reinforced when embarking on a future focused on designing buildings. For, theories about life had, indeed, to work in very practical ways on construction sites and then in the completed scheme, often for long periods of time. If they did not work, structures could collapse, people could be hurt and even be killed.

For, any answers had to lead to solutions that were able to be built and, literally, be inhabited. Theories had, therefore, to be ideas and thought frameworks that were reliable, with outcomes as places that could be lived in with confidence by people.

It is probable that you have asked questions that may be similar during your own life's journey. If so, you may already have other answers to ones that I will table. You may also have different theories about life that you have applied in your own experience of practice. Your known and tested answers may be far more helpful to others than mine, especially in your own arena. Once again, please do share those insights and experiences. For, we all need to hear what is evidence-based and, hence, what can be seen to work in practice. That is, if we are to respond to the challenge we face with positivity. From there, discussion and debate, with solidly reliable action following, is, literally, vital.

Such debate and application will, I am sure, need to be as vast and as far ranging as it is urgent. For, no arena in life is irrelevant. Every dimension, past, present and future will need to be considered and explored. As I have suggested, the need for confidence about life's present and past, including life's beginning, takes on a new urgency as we all move ever closer to a global end. That need for clarity will apply not just to our Earth, although that is huge. It will also need to apply to our cosmos. It, therefore, applies to the seemingly limitless, just as it does to our own seemingly small roles in life. All are parts of that one ever-larger macro picture.

With that in mind, allow me now to tell you a little more about how it was that I came to be me. Do then imagine the spiral-in process that I have already highlighted. For, a more personal insight could provide a deeper context that is relevant to the huge themes I will then explore. Allow me, therefore, to affirm that my own life is in the context of the lives of specific people living in a place and at specific points in our Earth's flow of history. Do also compare notes as part of a shared journey.

When the photograph in Image 7 was taken, I was in my early childhood years. My family's home was in Darlington in the northeast of England. Before I was born, my mum had difficulty conceiving. Dad then learned that the unmarried daughter of a good friend was pregnant. Knowing of the problems that might generate for those involved, especially in the mid-1940s, my parents asked if they could adopt the child. That was agreed before the birth. The prospect of adoption, I am sure, then enabled my own conception. As a result, my sister, Barbara, was born in February and I in October of 1947.

Image 8: A slightly older Ray, with his special sister, Barbara

As soon as we were old enough to understand, our mum and dad told Barbara and me of her adoption. They did so, when affirming that she had been doubly welcomed into our family. I grew, therefore, knowing that if her context had been different, I may not have been conceived. That helped me become aware that, if I had not then been born, I would not be in the photographs in any of the images so far. Nor would I now be aged 72 (!). As a result, I would not now be facing the same issue you are facing concerning a personal and global end.

Inevitably, I would also not be able to tell you something of my own life's journey, when seeking an understanding of the answer to the question 'why?' Just as there was a context for my own conception and birth, so the same principle applies to all our beginnings and everything else that follows.

Allow me to take that observation further. For, if there had also not been a flow of history up to the point of my conception, unless I have missed something, I would not have written these paragraphs and you would not be reading them (!). You may be thinking that this is obvious, which, in a sense, it is. However, what can seem obvious can, indeed, sometimes be overlooked. Allow me, therefore, to add another observation that is also obvious.

It is that I had nothing to do with the context that led to my birth, nor did I have anything to do with how, when and where I was conceived. I came into being, not because of my own actions, nor because of my own intentions. It happened because of other people, their actions and, from there, their own reasons why in their own lives. They, in turn, were part of a flow of history that started long before even they lived.

When recognising that ever larger context, let me be specific. For, I came into being, not only because of the lives of my mum and my dad, it was also because of my dear sister. Together, they were my three-as-one people-based context, all of whom lived within a bigger context. Without them and it, I would not be alive. As a result, my very existence is totally dependent upon people and a context that happened before my own conception and, hence, before my own beginning. I am highlighting this in order to point to a theme that will be pivotal as we journey forward. It is that my life is in the context of a flow of history that started well before my own. The same principle then applies to you, just as it does to everyone. A question then rises. It is:

. Was there also a context for the start of the whole of life?

I will quickly say that that question is gathered with every other question in the Summary at the end of this Step One. All those questions will be answered as we journey forward Step by Step.

Returning to exploration here, I would not exist without a flow of history as a context that involves deeply personal events and relationships experienced by others. There would not have been a 'me' that could ask questions and table insights into answers, in the way that I am here. There would not have been a 'me' that could then focus on what is perhaps the biggest question of all, namely, 'Life, what on Earth is it all about?'

There would also not be a 'you' that could do the same.

In order to exist, my life and your life, as well as my context and your context are, therefore, totally dependent on other people. The same principle then applies to any ability any of us has to ask and seek answers to questions about life. I am also 100% certain that the same observation of a context applies to everyone alive now and who has ever lived. As a result, to be able to ask and seek answers to fundamental questions about why we and the whole of life exists is then a form of gift given to us all. It is also a privilege that is rooted in a flow of history that had a beginning and is now moving toward an end.

For, everyone and, by implication, every living being has a context that is in the past. It is also a context in which we had no say. We can only know what it is by trusting other people who were there and who were able to remember and record what happened. My birth certificate is then a confirmation of both my birth and, whatever number of weeks before, my conception. Those factual contexts then impact on who I am and who we are in our personal, as well as our shared, lives in the years that followed, on into our present. One without the other is impossible. Without a degree of trust in memories and records, with a resultant confidence in the past, the only way we could journey forward into the future is by 'flying blind'.

Let me now take that 'flying blind' analogy a little further.

If we are to understand why it is that an end to life here on Earth is coming toward us:

a. A reliable understanding about how our past led to our present is crucial. As a result;

b. Being confident about our past is vital if we are to understand our present and why our future is as it is. It is only then that;

c. Our onward journey can be anticipated with any sense of a context that is real.

Without that past to future realism, we would, indeed, be simply be 'flying blind'. If it is that we are 'flying blind', my expectation is avoidable outcomes will lead to an end that will come in a more accelerated form. It would follow a degree of unnecessary chaos that could be very destructive. As a result:

a. Our personal and shared past, present and future are fully entwined and:

b. What remains of life must be understood with an urgency and a depth, perhaps as never before.

As we journey through these pages, I will highlight other seemingly obvious facts about life. A much bigger and ever relevant picture will then start to build. For, each insight will be akin to a hand that opens, awaiting a ball to catch of an answer of answers. Each observation will apply to me, just as it could, I am sure, also apply to you. Indeed, that application may be relevant to many others like me and you.

I will highlight each by using words. As I have suggested, I will also use photographs, as well as other images, like the ones already shown. You will also see the key role that diagrams have played in my journey, such as ones in Image 5 that spiral-in and spiral-out. You may have equivalent photographs and scrapbook memories that tell of the many situations in which you have found yourself. You may also have your own diagrams. If so, do get them out and use them to trace and understand your own flow of history, as I continue to unwrap mine.

As you have and will see, with my memories, there will come stories. You will also have stories to tell about people and places, with each giving an insight into your own life's journey. Once again, if you have not already done so, do feel able to write them down and then ponder each in parallel with my own. My expectation is that you may then find that many of the insights and principles that I will outline are also known in your own life. My expectation then is that you will also be able to identify with many of my experiences, just as I will yours. Indeed, that is one of the reasons why I am mentioning my background and experience. For, it is not only to help me, it is also that such remembering may help you discern what it is that makes your life special. With those insights, you may then be able to help me as well as many others too.

As you have seen, one of my early conclusions was that we are, indeed, all unique and, from there, we are all special. We may not feel comfortable in saying that, but it is a fact of life. There is no one else the same as me. I am, as a result, unique and special and the same applies to you.

When I look at my life's journey, I am very aware that a seed in my mother's womb grew to become the shy boy in Image 7, nestling into his mum's skirt.

That boy then changed in a small number of years to become the lad in Image 8. He can be seen in a jumper mum had knitted. I was taller and physically different, but I was still me. My hair was reasonably groomed, unlike that of the young man in the preceding Image 6. The photograph in Image 1 is then proof that I have since been to a hairdresser (!). As I write, the Coronavirus lockdown has meant that my hair needs attention again. Nevertheless, in the many decades since my younger days, I know that I am still me, with a lot of life lived and haircuts in between.

I am also now closer to my life's end than ever before. So much so that I am 100% certain that the time remaining is far less than that experienced since my seed beginning. A lot has inevitably happened along the way, just as it has in all our lives. All those changes are part of our individual life's flow of history. For each one of us, there have been a multitude of such changes. Yet, I am confident in saying that I have remained me, just as you have remained you. With the same principle applying to all of us. Once again, a seed to maturity and then an end is an obvious statement to make, but sometimes the obvious can be overlooked, with its significance not being seen. Having noted it, my desire was then to find out why it is part of an increasingly evident language in life.

. Why, therefore, am I highlighting these consistencies, with each being seemingly obvious, so early on our journey?

It is because:

a. Change over time is part of life, as is:

b. The thread of a consistent identity that has a beginning and that will have an end.

Both you and I are examples of those observable and evidence-based consistencies. Yet, by being obvious, each can easily be in danger of not being key to understanding why life is as it is. As a result, each can then not be seen to be directly relevant to the biggest questions we can ask. From there, they can be excluded from crucial answers that are now increasingly needed.

As a result, the answer to the big questions I am addressing must explain why it is that those, as well as other, observable facts are so intrinsically part of life here on Earth. For, by being part of life, they must be directly relevant to all the questions I asked and the answers I was seeking.

Allow me now to go another step further and highlight one more observable fact. It was one of which I was very aware when as a student, with my work life before me. It was also one that was as intriguing as it was obvious. It is:

The importance of places in time

For, none of us can live without being who we are in a place.

Today, the place I am occupying is a study in my home, which is a house in Witney, a market town in Oxfordshire. Even when I leave what I call my 'Man Cave', I am still in a place. It may be the lounge or garden of the house in the street that my wife, Jenny, and I occupy and call home. I may then be in the home of a friend. I may also be in a nearby shop. Wherever I am, I am in a place. If I was not in a place, I would not be here on planet Earth in the cosmos. Being me and being in a place are two phenomena that are, therefore, inseparable.

I then realised that there is more. For, none of us can live without being alive at a point in time. For, in order to be able to be alive as a person in a place, I must occupy time. I must not only have a context in the lives of specific people in the past. I must also have a context in my own, as well as our shared, flow of history.

My parents were part of my time context as people. They were key to my beginning. From the moment of my conception, as well as theirs, there was always another context. It was time. Just as they could only live in the context of people and a place, so, they could only be alive by being in a location in a flow of history that is made up of time. The same principle then applied to me. As a result, people and places are intrinsic parts of a flow of history that comprises time. It is a three-as-one people-place-and-time relationship that embraces everyone alive now and everyone that has ever lived. We are all then part of an even bigger flow of history that is relevant to every dimension of our Earth within its cosmos. So much so that their many relationships reach out into the seeming limitlessness of that vast context.

Another obvious fact in life follows on from the observation that each person, place and even planet is unique. It is that they each can have names that tell of how special they are. The same principle applies to time.

Just as I have a name and my home has a postal address, so the time context that I inhabit has a unique identity. When I first typed this sentence, it was originally December 16th, 2018, at 8.05 p.m. As I check through what I had written, it is now July 21st, 2020, at 5.40 p.m. I could also add 'and 27 seconds' (!). That specific moment will never come again, nor will every individual minute, hour, day or year.

Many writers have imagined physically stepping out of being a specific person, in a specific place at a specific point in time. They have also imagined entering another context either in the past or the future. There have even been popular television series based on that goal. As far as I am aware, that notion has only ever been imagined. It has never come about as a material reality. Unless I have missed something, no one has yet been able to step outside of who they are in their own context in time.

That time-based phenomenon is, therefore, a constraint that is part of who we are as people living in life. It is as specific as our parental and place-based contexts. All three have provided a framework for the lives we are privileged to live. Many people may have wanted to escape that constraint, but none has achieved it. If I am wrong in saying this, do let me know.

With that in mind as part of my own journey, my question soon became 'why?' for each of these 'obvious', evidence-based facts about life concerning people, places and time. I then came to a series of early conclusions. They were that:

a. I can only be me;

b. I cannot be anyone else;

c. I can only be me in one place. For, I cannot be in two places at once and:

d. I can only be me in that one place at specific points in time.

I also concluded that, even though the context of place and time will change, I would still be me. Albeit me that was and is, I trust, still learning and growing in a multitude of ways. I, therefore, also concluded that in life:

a. It is impossible for me to live without inhabiting the constraints of who I am, where I am and when I am.

Crucially, this then led me to further conclude:

b. That the answer to the question why about the whole of life would make sense of those evidence-based, obvious and observable phenomena.

What was then intriguing was another fact of life.

It was that every person in every place cannot stop time doing what time does. In essence, 'Time waits for no man'. For, time moves forward. It does so not only without stopping. It also does so irreversibly. In my own life, 'the march of time' is then the context for my own beginning and my own end. I am also certain that is the case for all human beings, as well as every other living being. As you can see, by quoting two well known phrases, many people have come to the same conclusion. That realisation then added even more urgency to the observation that time, it would seem, is moving irreversibly forward toward the end of life here on Earth.

One consequence was that the relevancy of the question 'why?' kept growing. It was focused on our Earth's life now:

a. Set in the context of its beginning;

b. The forward movement of time and:

c. When knowing that an end in time is ahead for us all, including the life of our Earth.

I then wondered whether the same principles applied to our host cosmos. My assumption steadily became that they did apply. The implications are then vast. For me, they literally took my breath away.

At this point, having highlighted time limits and 'ends', I feel I should add something positive. That is because there is the danger that the journey so far through these pages may give the impression of only negativity about our Earth's future. In order to affirm positives as well, the five extracts in Images 9, 10 and 11 are from articles that tell of projects and actions taken by individuals and groups of people. They are very practical responses to our local and global predicaments.

In the context of a huge negative, the need for positivity is vital. Otherwise, giving up can be the outcome and I am not about giving up. It is simply not an option. I say that because, before us all, is a reason for living that makes every moment precious and one full of opportunity. It is the opportunity to discern and then live life's reason for being.

Ethiopia plants 200 million trees in one day

By Elias Meseret
IN ADDIS ABABA

Ethiopia has claimed a world record for planting more than 200 million trees in a day.

The mass planting yesterday forms part of prime minister Abiy Ahmed's aims to help restore the country's landscape, which experts say is fast being eroded by deforestation and climate change.

The state-affiliated Fana Broadcasting Corporate announced more than 224 million trees were planted yesterday, surpassing the initial goal of 200 million trees planted in one day.

"Today Ethiopia is set in our attempt to break the world record together for a green legacy," the prime minister's office tweeted. Early yesterday, Mr Abiy planted trees in Ethiopia's southern region.

Ethiopia is in the midst of a tree planting campaign in which it aims to plant four billion trees between May and October. Agriculture officials stated that so far more than 2.6 billion trees, indigenous species, have been planted in 1,000 sites across the East African nation.

Earlier this month a group of Swiss scientists said that mass tree-planting was the most effective way to fight global warming. But they said another trillion or more would be needed.

The effort aims to beat the previous planting record, held by India

They estimated in the journal *Science* that this number of trees, covering an area equivalent to the USA, could suck up nearly 750 billion tonnes of heat-trapping carbon dioxide from the atmosphere. That is as much carbon pollution as humans have generated in the past 25 years.

According to Farm Africa, a forest management organisation in Ethiopia, less than four per cent of the country's land is now forested, a sharp decline from around 30 per cent at the end of the 19th century. Ethiopia's rapidly growing population and the need for more farmlands, unsustainable forest use and climate change are often cited as the causes for rapid deforestation.

Various international organisations and the business community have joined the tree planting spree, which aims to smash India's 66 million tree-planting record set in 2017.

It is not yet clear if Guinness World Records is monitoring Ethiopia's mass planting but the prime minister's office said that new software is helping with the count. AP

{i} Critics of Mr Abiy say he is using the campaign to distract from the challenges he is facing, including **ethnic conflicts** which have forced some 2.5 million people from their homes.

Image 9: Millions of trees are being planted

It is a reason for being that has profoundly personal, as well as practical, implications that can affect every one of us. That effect is then one that can be societal at every level of our global community. That means in every home, street, town, city, region, nation and continent on, as well as even beyond, our Earth. Do hang in, therefore, and be encouraged to never give up.

Net zero by 2050? Let's get to 30 by 30

The UK is now committed to a zero carbon society by 2050. But would it be wise to set a '30-by-30' target as Theresa May suggested just two years ago?

What is this? Put simply, a firm commitment and programme to ensure that around 27m homes and 3m non-residential buildings will be made completely energy efficient. Completed by 2030. Hence the slogan: 30 by 30.

Andrew Warren is chairman of the **British Energy Efficiency Federation**

Modi hails tiger conservation plan as roaring success

By Adam Withnall
IN DELHI

The number of tigers living in the wild in India has jumped to almost 3,000, an increase of almost a third in four years.

The surge in numbers thanks to conservation efforts, means India is now home to more than 70 per cent of the world's wild tiger population.

Presenting the figures, Prime Minister Narendra Modi called it a "historic achievement".

"With around 3,000 tigers, India has emerged as of one of the biggest and safest habitats for them in the world," Mr Modi (*inset*) said, praising all the stakeholders involved in the country's tiger conservation exercise.

"Nine years ago, it was decided in St Petersburg that the target of doubling the tiger population would be 2022. We in India completed this target four years in advance," Mr Modi said.

India counts its tigers once every four years, and has been achieving modest increases since the population dwindled to just 1,400 in 2005.

The count in 2014 was 2,226, said environment minister Prakash Javadekar. For 2018, it rose to 2,967, with a margin of error of about 350.

The survey was led by the National Tiger Conservation Authority, and the Wildlife Institute of India, and carried out on an unprecedented scale. A total of 381,400 sq km of forests were surveyed, with camera traps deployed on a 2 sq km grid and forest department staff walking a combined 522,996km.

The Global Tiger Forum, an inter-governmental body co-ordinating tiger conservation across the Asian countries that are home to them, said the "scale of the assessment is unparalleled globally".

Dr Yadvendradev Jhala, the lead scientist for the count, said tiger numbers had gone up significantly in areas which experts previously believed had reached their maximum capacity.

"The population has gone up... We didn't expect this, but it has, and that's incredible," he said.

WWF India, which assisted with the count, said the survey results should "bring both great hope and reassurance about the tigers' prospects".

The tiger is India's national animal, and since the 1970s around 5 per cent of the country's total land mass has been designated as national parks for the purpose of protecting them and other endangered species.

THE INDEPENDENT

{i} **Tigers mostly eat deer and wild boar**, but have occasionally been known to kill people, too. This usually happens when a tiger is old or sick and unable to catch its normal prey.

Image 10: Two more timely encouragements

For, even when still seeking out life's reason why, everyone can do something that is personal, practical and special, with each as a positive contribution to addressing the negative issue I am – and we all are – facing. It is one that will not go away. Many people are already responding with practical positivity and they are doing so whilst there is still time. By facing the scale of that negative, my goal is to do the same. It is to be practical by contributing as positively as possible to life's flow of history. It is also to do so in the context of a clear insight into life's reason why.

As we journey forward through these pages, I will give you more examples of my own responses as a designer of places, including several when working with others. I will do so, once again, because my overall goal is to make a positive contribution, when facing the negative implicit in THE BIGGEST CHALLENGE ever to be faced by humanity.

My own reason for being positive may surprise you. Indeed, your reason for doing the same may surprise me. That is the privilege of sharing. Whatever that reason, my trust is that the newspaper and magazine cuttings in Images 9 and 10 will be encouragements. You will be able to add your own, including ones that are more recent.

Those articles give insight into some of the many responses so far to the predicament we all now face. As a result, they are also the context for who I am and who we all are as people in places and time. That context includes events and experiences that have helped shape the way we think and, from there, how we respond to situations and issues. That context also includes insights across generations and hence:

a. The insights tabled by Sir David Attenborough, as someone greatly valued and older than I, as well as:

b. Greta Thunberg, as a remarkable woman, who is much younger.

The further articles in Images 11a and 11b then give an insight into the remarkable contribution to this debate.

Those articles give insight into some of the many positive responses when facing a negative.

Allow me now to add another of my own responses. It is that, if what life is all about only has a context that was negative, I would not have started writing these many pages. I would not be highlighting who I am and who we all are. I would also not be specific about observations concerning people, places and time that have helped shape the way I think and, from there, how I respond to

The brighter side of climate change

IT WAS so refreshing to see "the most trusted man in Britain" call out world leaders over their cynical attitude to climate change – in particular naming and shaming the USA and Australia.

And the great thing is, Sir David Attenborough, while not mincing his words at a Westminster committee hearing, does not peddle negativity.

He is adamant that tackling climate change is possible, could be tremendous fun and that if countries like ours get ahead of the game, we could create economic growth, and some could even make a fortune.

Perhaps we should all become tree surgeons or foresters. Look at how that business is set to boom, with plans to plant three billion trees in the next three decades here in the UK. Not just in forests but on derelict spots, old industrial land, hedgerows and perhaps our back gardens.

The British government has committed to reducing greenhouse gas emissions to zero by 2050 and a huge part of achieving that is a tree-planting revolution.

I've done my bit. I have a pocket handkerchief of a garden but I have planted eight trees and they are a delight, each quietly getting on with being carbon absorbing instead of carbon emitting. They're tall, green, oxygen machines. Everyone with a garden should plant a tree. Though you should consult an expert on the type and growth size first.

Perhaps one day, when driverless cars can be summoned at the tap of an app, we will become a nation who no louger own cars and will therefore no longer need garages. So we can plant a tree in every garage plot.

Surely clever governments should see the financial benefits of a "space-race" type mission to be the world leader at backing the sort of science and technology that will help heal the planet. Remember, the space race gave us ear thermometers, scratch-resistant glasses, space blankets, freeze-dried food, and even the Dustbuster.

Scientists and engineers can get us out of this ecological mess we've created. That's not complacency talking. It's faith, in human potential. But it's got to be backed by big money, and global dedication.

There's a little island off Madeira, Porto Santo, that's becoming the first energy independent island by eliminating the use of fossil fuels. Renault has created a smart car which generates and stores electricity not just to drive but to release back into the national grid every evening, when demand goes up. Attenborough, who is a self-confessed frequent fly assured the committee that scientists will one day give us electric planes so we can still go on holiday. But while we hang on Attenborough's every word, Donald Trump couldn't care less.

And Australia's policy decisions suggest their leaders are climate-change sceptics despite it being home to astonishing natural diversity from the koala to the already ecologically damaged Great Barrier Reef. They seem more interested in propping up their coal and natural gas industries.

Their stubborn refusal to embrace a healthier future is unethical – and dangerous for us all.

Sir David told MPs: "I have been speaking with the international finance bodies and it is clear to them that actually this is an opportunity to get things right, this is an opportunity to make big profits and to innovate new systems. If we're ahead of the game, we'll benefit from it."

As the generation of children currently protesting every Friday become politicians themselves, we'll have an adult generation that cares – even if those in power right now don't. Tackling climate change is not all doom and gloom, it can be exciting. If only people such as Donald Trump could see that.

WARNING: But Attenborough says innovation brings benefits

Image 11a One more

situations and issues. That context includes and has benefited from the insights tabled by Sir David Attenborough and Greta Thunberg, as well as those of many others.

They, in turn, have their own contexts, with each overlapping with mine as well as yours. Together, we are all then contributors to an increasingly highly focused era in our Earth's history, as part of an ongoing flow of history. It is one that journeys from some form of beginning to an end that will be personal, relational and rooted in places all over our Earth. It is one where we are 'in this together'. It is also one constrained by time that is ticking away, with a limited number of seconds, minutes, days and years remaining.

What is then noticeable in these observations is that all are finite. All exist and all are specific. They are also not just theoretical ideas. Each is real. As a result, my own time limit is moving from a beginning towards an end. When that end comes, I will not be visible in a place, nor will I be alive in the time sequence that governs our lives. As I have affirmed, that personal end to my finiteness may not be far away. Yours is also finite and will be doing the same.

Don't pick on Greta – she's an inspiration to the whole world

The environmental campaigner and Nobel Prize nominee Greta Thunberg has incurred the ire of an Australian right-wing columnist, who writes that she is "freakishly influential... a deeply disturbed messiah", and a "priestess of the cult" of "climate panic".

Andrew Bolt's highly personal column in the Murdoch-owned tabloid *Herald Sun* drew particular condemnation for focusing on the fact that the Swedish teenager has been diagnosed with Asperger's syndrome, a form of autism.

The 16-year-old campaigner (left) has just announced that she is embarking on an emission-free trip across the Atlantic to speak at a UN climate summit in September, hitching a ride on a high-tech racing yacht fitted with solar panels and underwater turbines which generate zero-carbon electricity.

Bolt rants about Greta's "unwillingness to compromise" and "totalitarian certainty". "I have never seen a girl so young and with so many mental disorders treated by so many adults as a guru," he claims, adding: "Her intense fear of the climate is not surprising from someone with disorders which intensify fears."

Australia, by contrast, is utterly conflicted about the environment. The aggressive mining and trucking lobbies have seen railways decline and close, with the majority of goods moved by road. Meanwhile, new mining franchises are approved and wind and solar energy is still at the starting gate.

In a week when Google's conference on global warming in Sicily was attended by hundreds of celebrities (and – allegedly – Prince Harry) arriving in 114 private jets, it's not surprising that Greta Thunberg attracts such ire.

She is the real thing, a charismatic inspirational figure who will not compromise. And that is her attraction to hundreds of thousands of people.

THE INDEPENDENT

@The_Real_JSP

Image 11b And another

These are facts of life that must be faced as a pivotal part of any question 'why?' If they are not then addressed and integral to any answers tabled, my conclusion was that those answers will be ultimately of no lasting value. Allow me, therefore, to summarise before going further, by using my own life as an example.

a. The babe that was born to my parents in 1947 is finite;

b. I am alive because of a context that I did not initiate;

c. That context is now part of the life I live today;

d. I grew from a child and will not live forever. I am going to die. I do not know when that end will come, but I know it will happen and;

e. I am also 100% sure that, just as you too were born, you are finite and will die.

Finitude, with a beginning and an end, is indeed one of life's certainties. That is why it must not be sidelined or lessened in terms of relevancy. It must be part of any answer to questions about why life exists. If it is not, then, for me at least, answers are not based on reality and hence must be fully and justifiably challenged and set aside.

I am emphasising those core facts about life now, not only because they must be faced, but also because they then lead to some other core questions, including:

. Why are those finite contexts and constraints so immovably there?

. Why is life only able to be lived in the context of finite people, places and time?

. Why do these contexts have within them the inevitability of an end in death?

As a necessary point of emphasis, do note the importance of that small word 'why'. Even our ability to ask a question deserves a 'why?' For, the very existence of evidence-based 'science' starts with a positive, enquiring and expectant 'why?' Some might also say that what are called 'the arts' are then a way of expressing any insights and answers gained. The journey now unfolding through these pages is, therefore, towards a positive 'science' and 'arts' based answer to every question, including ones that start with that crucial word, 'why'.

As our spiral-in journey continues, allow me to now tell you a little more about my own early years.

For, after my birthplace in Darlington, my people and place context changed. It was when my family moved to a different location. It too had a name and was a town called Middlesbrough in what was then known as the North Riding of Yorkshire. Darlington was a market town. My new home was regarded as an industrialised port. My dad had worked in a Co-op grocery store and my mum in a post office. When moving to Middlesbrough, they bought a corner shop in an area known, rather quaintly, as 'Brambles Farm'. The farm, however, had ceased to exist, with the name becoming that of a pub opposite the shop and with an ice cream factory alongside. We moved there when I was five and lived above mum and dad's workplace up to me being ten.

Like so many of our relatives, my parents had decided to emigrate, with the goal of a more stable future for a growing family. Australia was that place of opportunity. We were to travel on what was called, 'a ten-pound ticket', heavily subsidised probably by both the UK and Australian governments. I can remember dad driving us south to board a ship in Southampton. Before we reached our destination, he became ill. The place from which we were to embark then became my home from age 11 to 18, when I travelled to London as a student. Some 25 locations in London became my temporary places of abode. That was before I met Jenny, when Lewisham in southeast London became our home for 38 years. We then moved to Witney in Oxfordshire some seven years ago.

Darlington, Middlesbrough, Southampton and a number of other communities comprising people and places in London – all were different and special, before another specific place became a home here in Witney. So far, that journey has taken 72 years.

Soon after becoming a student in London, I went on another much shorter journey. It was to the USA and then to Canada. On that occasion, it was not with the goal of moving home. It was to see the many pavilions that showcased the identity and achievements of nations from around the world. All were people living in places in time. Each was then part of, what was called, Expo 67. Its host city was Montreal. I flew to New York. With a Greyhound bus ticket that cost 99 dollars for unlimited use for 99 days, I travelled to Toronto before Montreal, then to Vancouver and eventually down the west coast of North America to California. It was there that I sat on my first surfboard, intent on riding the Pacific waves before me. Throughout, I was getting ready for a future now beginning to unfold.

As in the image on the front cover, I remember looking out to sea, imagining what could soon be. Some minutes later, reality struck as I realised how difficult it can be to stay on a surfboard when trying to ride the waves! Moments of anticipated success were then followed by frequent failure. You may know what I mean. Having said that, you may also be an expert surfer (!).

Wipe out

I am highlighting this sequence, when facing the waves that are coming toward us all here on planet Earth. Within the biggest is the huge question that I have raised, as well as many associated questions rooted in observations of life. Each embraces people and places, as well as time. Dimensions that then unite all three are the importance of identity, relationships and, from there, that precious sense that I have highlighted. It is a sense of belonging. All are then set in the context of the seeming inevitability of death.

There is a sense in which anticipating the exhilaration of riding a wave before, to use a surfing term, 'wipe out' occurs seems to summarise those contradictions. Having suggested that, if 'wipe out' meant death and not just an opportunity to try again, my expectation is that the sport would be banned. As a result, we enjoy danger, but dying is one step too far. That principle then applies, not only to human beings, but also to the amazing, yet precarious, life of our Earth.

As a result, when still as a student, an early lesson was that a beginning, a belonging and then an end are fundamental parts of life's journey. I have since come to see that the same principle applies to every living being, from insects to birds and from plants to trees. Each is an integral part of an all-embracing dynamic within life that is based on the same principles here on planet Earth.

So much has happened since that formative experience when holding a surfboard in 1967, with many more insights gained. Nevertheless, it was, for me, as generic as it has been spot-on target. That is why I have included a surfer on the front cover here. For, there have been times when my own subsequent journey has been as exhilarating as it has been tumultuous. I now know what it feels like 'to ride a wave' in many contexts. I also know what it is like 'to be deluged in wipe out' and disorientated by many more waves.

I am sure you will be able to identify with those 'ups' and 'downs' experiences in your own unique ways as well. Allow me, therefore, to ask another sequence of questions, with each beginning with a now familiar word. Answers will follow. Those questions are:

. Why is life, not just constrained by personal identities, place and time, but also full of seeming extremes of exhilaration and tumult and with so many in-betweens?

. Why do I, as well as no doubt we, prefer the 'ups' and not the 'downs'?

. Why do we, seemingly inevitably, experience both?

My life so far has embraced seven decades of seeking to ride my own life's big wave, with its many smaller waves along the way. I have succeeded, as well as fallen off, my surfboard and have done so on many occasions. Along the way a clear sequence of themes has, for me, come through. They are that, alongside a beginning and an end, with time in between, all lives have:

a. A reference point that is as sensitive as it can be dynamic. I have already declared its primacy. It is that life is all about 'belonging' and;

b. That the same insight may also apply to all other living beings as well.

As a result, when addressing the many questions that are now gathering, my core goal became to set a framework for answering the following, with each set in the context of exhilarations and tumults, beginnings and ends:

. What is belonging?

. Why is belonging so important in all our lives?

. What is the dynamic of belonging in the day to day lives of people and places?

. How can I then enable a sense of belonging when designing places?

All those questions were as practical as the work arena I was entering. All my answers, therefore, had to be equally practical. Add to that the reason why I have used the phrase 'The Last Millennium', my goal then is that each answer would become a contribution to a debate about the biggest 'wave' of all.

It is important now to confirm that those answers are merely my own. It is also when knowing that its various themes have been tested in my work arena in the five decades since my surfboard experience, with each being highly practical. As you know, they were of Architecture and Planning, as well as more recently, what I call, 'development facilitation'. That last phrase means having ideas for major projects and seeking to help each come into being. You have glimpsed what that involves. I will show you more examples as we journey forward.

A key point to emphasise now is that all the examples, whether as scheme designs or as project strategies, are very practical. Each is deliberately intended as a positive response to THE BIGGEST CHALLENGE we all face. It is for you then to discern how beneficial or otherwise that has been. Do then let me know your response. I will also give my own assessment of each project. For, once again, my goal is simply to learn. Even within the limited time remaining, it is then to be as effective as I can in my own response to that challenge.

For, I am very aware that I think and live through the medium of, what is still, an emerging world view. We are all in the same situation, even if we may not realise it is happening. If you are not already aware of that, do, please, note it as a proposal to consider. Do then feel able to set out your own way of seeing the world and apply it as part of your own critique of my world view theory outworked in practice. For, you will then be able to test not only my response, but also your own as a valued contribution to THE BIG DEBATE now so urgently needed.

If you are willing to do that, allow me now to thank you.

As a result, my goal through these pages is a form of 'sharing' that can lead to a dialogue, debate and with positive action following. For, my reference point is deadly serious for each one of us, individually and as a global community.

I am very aware that I am taking a risk when doing so, but it is a necessary one. By reading this far, thank you also for taking a risk as well.

Heading Four

A BOY BECAME A MAN

Image 12: Ray and Jenny by the River Thames, not far from its source

When Southampton was home, the River Itchen and the Solent became part of my belonging. When in London, the River Thames was ever present

My home is now near Oxford, close to its source

As you will see all those waterways now host projects

All are about belonging as a response to the deadly serious predicament we all face

As well as my own understanding of the reason why for life

I will now spiral into more detail by telling you of an early success in the context of a sense of belonging. It then became an agonised failure when that belonging was lost. The reason for both is known by many other people.

For, before my surfboard experience as my architectural studies approached, a deep belonging that I had known over four years with a girl came to an unexpected end. The pain I felt was intense. As a result, I have deep sympathy for anyone who has known such a loss, whether in their teens or at any stage in their lives. For many, four years is small, with relationships ending after many decades. That can make the pain of their loss even harder to bear. That is especially when the opportunity for new belongings often reduces with age. In amongst my own youthful inner turmoil, I knew, nevertheless, that I had my adult life ahead.

That is why I decided to learn from that experience. As a result, my focus became seeking answers to an ever-growing list of questions 'why?' An early one, perhaps inevitably, was:

. Why does a broken relationship lead to pain?

And then:

. Why is pain so painful?

I was in my late teens. I then began to realise that those questions were part of the much bigger sequence of questions I am seeking to answer here. As a result, the early insights I gained framed my approach to my studies. Each then informed my lifetime's work as a designer of places for people. Each insight enabled me to see an ever-bigger picture concerning life itself, with a spiralling-in and spiralling-out being the consequence.

As you have seen, many questions began to pour forth that also needed answers. This was not only to each specifically, but also to all as part of one overall world view. You may have known equivalent turmoil, as well as pain. Yours may have come at a similar age, or during a different era in your life. Your response may also have been to ask questions, with some of my own included. For me, each question led to more as my desire to learn grew, starting with the sequence that I have already highlighted. It was also with me seeing each as needing an answer that was as clear as the observations I was noting. That sequence was:

. I have grown from being a child to being a young man. I am physically different, but why is the 'me' inside intrinsically still the same?

. Was that same 'me' also there as a seed in my mother's womb?

. If so, at whatever age, why am I consistently me?

A related question then came, which I wrestled with for many a month. I have alluded to it already, but now it was being asked with almost a demand for an answer, as it seemed to be so very fundamental. It was:

. Why am I not someone else?

Like many of my contemporaries, I was an ardent Beatle fan in my teens. Even in my 70s, I enjoy listening to their music. I vividly remember my sense of excitement when, in a sense, sharing in their lives and who they had become. For a while, I even modelled myself on John Lennon and wore round-rimmed spectacles, an Afghan coat and hair down to my shoulders. As a detail, I bought that coat in Istanbul, toward the end of the tour around islands in Greece, as photographed in Image 6. I may even have enjoyed the thought of being like him or even being him, but I knew that could never be.

For, I was me as myself and John Lennon was who he was as himself. Even he could not become another person. There may have been occasions when he may have wanted to be someone else, but, just as it was impossible for me, so it was the same for him. It may be that he even asked the further questions that I then asked myself. They were extensions of my last question and were:

. Why is it other people are themselves, not me?

. Why is it that we can all grow and change in so many ways, but nevertheless always remain intrinsically who we are?

. Why, therefore, am I an individual and as uniquely me as you are you?

And then, with a sense of intrigue:

. Have others asked those questions?

. Have people in every generation asked and sought answers when doing what I was doing, which was to simply note the way life is?

. Have, therefore, the questions I am asking here been raised throughout human history?

I could not prove it, but my own answer to the last three of those questions was, 'Yes, this appears to be the case. Such questions must have been, in some measure, part of everybody's life, no matter who, when or where'. On the assumption that was accurate, another question then arose, which was:

. Why is it that, generation after generation, we want to know answers to key questions and, indeed, any question?

As you have seen, certain questions were rooted in success as well as failure, belonging as well as pain. More questions followed, with many more answers sought. Having felt the joy of a positive relationship and the opposite when it was broken, I specifically wanted to understand:

. Why is it that relationships can lead to almost blissful happiness, as well as agony when lost?

. Why are relationships so important in the lives of people?

There was another related question. I had begun to realise that relationships, like people, could begin, succeed, then fail and even die. Those relationships were very tangible and existed almost as fully as I did. The girl I knew had not died, but the relationship we shared had. I then looked at my mum and dad and became very aware that an end to the life of each would not only inevitably come to each, it would also come to the relationship they shared. I then realised that, as individual people and as a relationship, they had protected me every year of my life. As a result, that anticipation of loss led me to feel very exposed. It was then as if everyone around me was touched with the inevitability of death, with pain then following.

In more recent years, my daughter, Claire, seemed to become aware of the same, when saying she wanted our shared lives to go on forever, but we both know they will not. Loss and pain will come.

As I typed those words, a song by Simon and Garfunkel went through my mind, with a phrase that summarises one response. They sang: 'I am a rock. I am an island. And an island feels no pain.'

The suggestion then is that not being able to enjoy a relationship is better than having to face the possibility of being hurt. In my own youthful years, I was tempted to think the same, but resisted. I was still a young man, with that surfboard and waves of a lifetime ahead of me. Nevertheless, I began to ask the question 'why are relationships so important?' It was a genuine inquiry. It was also in another context. For, I had also begun to realise that our Earth lives because of relationships, with our lives being possible because of lives that have gone before. Our Earth is now facing the prospect of an end to all relationships. It was then that I first asked:

. Why is death not just in human beings, but also in every dimension of life?

That question was, once again, followed by another that almost seemed absolute. I was on the threshold of a lifetime of opportunity, but nevertheless I had to ask:

. Why is it that, in life, death always seems to win?

It was during my teenage years that I found myself leaning toward becoming an Architect. That was because it seemed to be a positive arena in which I could help others relate together, with the goal of belonging in a place. I had not framed my goal quite as clearly as that, but that was what I was feeling toward. I had been hurt, but I was not depressed. I was intent on turning a negative experience into one that was positive. When I look back, the positivity always shown by my parents when facing adversity, as well as the ethos of the Grammar School I attended, were definite factors.

I was also aware that the answers to a steadily enlarging number of questions had to be relevant to my intended workplace. I began, therefore, to set my explorations in the context of my slowly emerging skills as a designer of places for people, whether as individuals or as groups. It was not long before I saw Architecture as a window into a much bigger way of seeing life. One consequence was the need to enlarge my own place-based theoretical arena. That led to my subsequent decision to study Planning. I also began to see every architectural scheme as having sub-schemes that embraced Interior Design.

That is why, after studying Architecture for five years and Planning for two, I focused on Interior Design and did so as part of my workplace activities. It was by serving actual clients that the importance of relationships became even more evident. They were abundant between the many people and organisations involved in the design and construction processes. There was also the constant possibility of a breakdown in relationships, with disputes arising. I, therefore, added another qualification, this time in Arbitration. It was with the goal of being better able to resolve potential disagreements, especially between the clients I served and the building contractors they employed.

All those practitioner arenas were, for me, set in the context of core questions about why life is as it is, including the many related questions I have begun to highlight here. Much of this was initially exploratory, but always in the context of a seriousness that then infused the work I was doing. As I journeyed forward, summary phrases helped me understand underlying themes that began to come into focus. I was very aware that I hardly knew what I was thinking, but one phrase I used, when studying Planning, was that:

LIFE IS ABOUT TIME, CHANGE, PAIN AND DEATH

Those early insights were as tantalising as they were also agonised. Nevertheless, it was through those deliberations that I was able to clarify my thinking as a designer of places both large and small. As you have seen, the seed had by then already been sown for my life's workplace goal, which was:

TO ENABLE A SENSE OF BELONGING FOR PEOPLE IN A PLACE

As you have also glimpsed, I focused on that statement because I had seen the positive effect of such a sense of belonging in the life of my family. I had also done so on a daily basis when observing my mum and dad in their workplace, a shop. I have introduced you to my mum, with me as a child. As part of a spiral-in process, allow me now to say a little more about my mum and dad and do so in the context of their early places of work.

My mum had worked in the post office and dad in the Co-op store in Darlington. Both institutions embodied an ethos of service in their community. In their different ways, each also had as their point of reference that of enabling a very practical sense of belonging. The group photograph in Image 13 is very much of its era. As a result, I value it immensely. Do note that everyone gathered is him or herself. They may all be wearing jackets, with all the men wearing ties, but their clothes hosted a person with each being unique and identifiably so. That is why I can recognise my dad as being in the centre of the 3rd row down.

Do also note that everyone assembled is smiling. That, for me, tells of that special quality that I have highlighted. It is that they enjoyed both being who they were and their sense of shared identity. Their resultant belonging was then, in part, because they did so around a core set of goals, as well as values. For, they shared a way of seeing the world that led to a desire to serve others.

Image 13: Staff of the Co-op in Darlington

Mum and dad met at a dance. After they married, they concluded to combine their customer focused skills in a more direct way by buying their own much smaller corner shop. Having set up my own architectural practice, when I look back at their endeavours, I am full of admiration for their courage when doing so. They took a huge risk and they succeeded. What I find remarkable is that they did so when their lives were somewhat full, to say the least. For, my sister and I were still children aged five years. We must have been a 'handful'. I have also wondered whether them running their own business, helped me be able to do the same. If so, 'Thank you, mum and dad.'

As you have seen, the shop they bought was in Middlesbrough. Their decision to migrate to Australia was not because their shop failed, because it was a success. It was for bigger family reasons. Dad becoming ill eventually led to my parents buying another corner shop in Southampton. On each occasion, my family lived 'above the shop'. Our home was, therefore, where my parents worked, not elsewhere. Home and work were a two-as-one. As a result, I grew being able to watch my parents, not only look after my sister and me in our home, I also saw them serve their customers. They did so in order to earn the income, penny by penny, to feed and clothe us.

There was then one key consequence that was as profound as it was subtle. So much so that I did not realise how relevant it was until after my relationship break-up in my late teens. For, week by week, I saw my mum and dad build a sense of belonging in their local community and they did so, specifically, through their workplace.

Each transaction was a way of earning a living for their family. As I watched, I realised that each was also about a relationship. Often in over-the-counter conversations, personal information was shared, with events in the streets around being noted. News items and ideas were explored, just as personal problems were discussed and even solved. For, my mum would often say to a customer in some distress, 'Come round to the kitchen and have a cup of tea.' I then knew that any difficulty being faced may soon have a solution.

As a result, in varying degrees each customer was a friend. I later concluded that my parents' shop was not only a place where they worked and earned a living, it was also one where:

PEOPLE RELATED TO PEOPLE

AND DID DO SO IN A RELATIONSHIP TOGETHER AS ONE

It was my early way of expressing an insight that I later knew had to be pivotal in my own lifetime goal of serving others. I would be using different workplace skills, but my intention was the same. Despite the clumsiness of that summary, you will find I will increasingly use refinements of those words in the pages which follow. There was then a further lesson that I will share with you that I have applied to myself. It is to value even an inadequate attempt to describe something that may be new and fledgling. Note it and then nurture it. Do so by understanding its meaning as theory and then test it by applying its implications in practice. If it is a lesson that you have already learned, I trust you do not mind me sharing it.

I also noted something else that I have since concluded is fundamental to any understanding about why life is as it is. It had an effect that led to a 'cold chill' feeling on many occasions.

For, especially when in Southampton, I grew knowing a look that would, at times, come on my dad's face. He always tried to hide it. One of the outcomes of living and working in one place is that hiding feelings can be impossible. For, it was almost inevitable that my sister and I would overhear occasional conversations that could be difficult.

I have used the phrase 'cold chill'. I could feel it on occasions as I listened and as I looked. It came when I heard my parents wrestle with stressful news that, in other families, might be distant. A ship that was expected to come into dock for repair had not done so. There would, therefore, not be work for many of the customers mum and dad served, who lived in the council estate across the road. The immediate effect was that many would not be able to pay for their groceries. The loss of income and the pain felt by others would then impact on my parents and, inevitably, also on my sister and me.

We all have different contexts in our lives. One that my parents lived with and had to face was vulnerability. As with so many small businesses, they could not control the bigger marketplace that their customers occupied. If jobs were lost, my parents would, inevitably, share the deeply felt pain of no income. For, as a customer suffered, so did mum and dad as local shopkeepers.

One consequence was that I grew with the phrase 'On tick' being well known. It meant that mum and dad were carrying the cost of purchases made by customers, with the risk of then not being paid. Despite that possibility, my mum and dad still helped. Despite the negative implications for our family, they still served. They did so because they loved others. One consequence was that their customers loved them in return. Together, they then built a sense of shared belonging as a community. It was when seeing their commitment to others that I knew that my own future workplace would be:

a. About earning an income, but also far more. It would be about serving others. As a result:

b. It would not be about 'my career', with an emphasis on the word 'my'. Indeed, in the decades since, the number of times I have used those two words can be counted using the fingers on one of my hands. Instead:

c. My work life would, at its core, be about serving, even when knowing that there may be no reward. It would then:

d. First and foremost, be about building a sense of community by designing places that enabled the sense of belonging I felt at home, in my parents' corner shop and in the streets where we lived. In order to be able to do that:

e. I had to earn, just as my mum and dad had to generate an income, but that was not my primary goal. Earning a living was, therefore, to be an enabler.

One further consequence was clarity concerning my work life. It was that it would, ultimately, not only not be about me, it would be about others. I knew I would not always succeed. I also knew that there would, at times, be a cost that would bring the same sense of 'chill' that I felt, when overhearing my mum and dad talking. Idealistic it may be, but that was my goal. It was first to enable a sense of belonging that would, in turn, be enabled by me earning a living.

As my life's focus became increasingly clear, I also knew that the pain my parents had, at times, felt would also apply to me. In the decades following, that came on many occasions, especially when recessions struck. The effect of each took years to recover from. So much so that my practice eventually had to close in 2007, after 34 years of trading. When that happened, not just the sense of chill, but the sheer weight of stress was crushing. This was especially when knowing that, not just my own, but several other families were dependent on my workplace succeeding. As a result my health failed and I could have died, as the pain my parents so often felt overwhelmed me.

Yet, throughout, I also knew that the privilege of enabling a shared belonging, by serving others, had been worth the risk of pain as well as eventual loss. That is why, when I look back, I am grateful for the early boy-girl relationship of belonging shared in my teenage years. The pain and loss I felt does not remove that precious memory. It has enabled me to always value beyond measure the relationship I now share with my Jenny.

As a result, I am grateful for the many experiences of success as well as failure in the several decades since. Both have come when seeking to enable a sense of belonging for others by designing places. Eventually in 2007, there was a cost that could have been terminal, but that cost was worth the positive outcomes along the way.

I trust you can see why I am highlighting cost alongside belonging. It is because cost is directly relevant to the huge challenge that we all now face. For, we have all wanted and known in some measure a sense of belonging. That is one of the privileges, when living in this our planetary home here on Earth. Yet, we are also all journeying into an ever more precarious personal and shared global future. We are facing a degree of loss that is almost beyond anyone's imagination. The cost is also real.

As a result, there is immense value in every moment when serving others by enabling that precious sense of belonging. Even in the context of cost and even only when as a memory, belonging is of immense value. I will come back to this more fully as we journey forward. For, I discovered that it is a crucial insight that led to me seeing and knowing the answer to the question, 'Life, what on Earth is it all about?'

In amongst many tears, therefore, there has also been an ever-deeper joy.

Loving people through a workplace

With cost as a backcloth, the word 'austerity' has become well known in the UK in recent years. It was an ever-present prospect for my parents and their customers. Another word is now also well-known. It is 'contagion', not least in the context of the Coronavirus pandemic around our world. Its negative implications have led, not only to the chills my parents felt, but also far worse. There is now the expectation that a severe economic recession will be a direct consequence of the need for lockdown.

In the northeast of England during my childhood era, an equivalent economic contagion had led to many seeking a more reliable future by migrating to other lands. For others, that was not a possibility. They had, in a sense, to face the prospect of decline every day. Despite that, I grew up seeing the generosity of so many people who had little. They helped neighbours who had even less. I was, therefore, deeply privileged to know that belonging in a community can lead to a form of hardship that is shared.

For, I saw how loss can result in a mutual support, appreciation and, from there, even a certain contentment. Heartfelt kindness can then follow, the value of which cannot be quantified in monetary terms. In our own era, the Coronavirus pandemic has radically changed our lives here in the UK, as well as around the world. Throughout, the same kindness has been evident. Many millions of people will, I am sure, join with me and say to everyone who has shown such practical kindness, 'A big thank you'.

As you will discover, I am saying that now, not only because it is justified in our current context, but also for another reason. It is because it will be crucial as the prospect of a dying Earth becomes ever more evident in our daily lives. For, it could herald by far the worst economic downturn ever in human history.

My privilege, therefore, has been to know that, even in difficult contexts, a care-based, sacrificial belonging can be experienced and valued every day. Kindness can be shown, no matter what the context. As a result, I am convinced it can still be the case everywhere, even when we are all facing the impending end to life here on Earth. Do, please, hold that thought. For, if the Coronavirus does become less dominant, kindness will be even more relevant when the issue of climate change and an endangered Earth return as national and global headlines. Indeed, when you read these pages that may have already happened.

When returning to my mum and dad's shop, I also grew watching the customers my parents served respond to the kindness and care they showed. One consequence was that my sister and I were part of an extended 'family', far bigger than just the Halls. We belonged in a community that looked out for us. They were also genuinely pleased that we belonged with them. Sometimes that meant that my parents learned very quickly of their son not behaving as he should (!). On other occasions, customers celebrated with me when I had succeeded, say, in gaining a place at a college in London to study Architecture.

Each was a practical outcome from a shared belonging that further reinforced my determination to enable a sense of belonging through my own work arena. Having seen evidence of it in the way my parents had lived and served others, it was, nevertheless, a dynamic that was hard to quantify. It was also one that was as tangible as it was and is fundamental. For, at its core is nothing less than the privilege of being able to love other people.

When I was later able to look back and remember my founding years, I then came to one clear and very privileged conclusion. It was that:

I GREW WATCHING MY PARENTS LOVE PEOPLE THROUGH THEIR WORKPLACE

It is thanks to them that I concluded to do that same. By then it was more than even enabling a sense of belonging using emerging design skills. It was, in the process, to love people. My own workplace was soon to be different to that of my mum and dad, yet the principle of serving and building a sense of belonging in a community was the same. It was, at its heart, by loving others and doing so in very practical ways.

I also slowly realised that what was ahead was a form of fulfilment. It was to be one, not just for me, but also specifically for my dad. For, I learned that he had wanted to become a draughtsman, but he was prevented from doing so by the economic difficulties the North East of England was facing. Perhaps, drawing and designing are in our shared DNA, but having a pencil in my hand came very naturally to me.

When in Middlesbrough, I remember drawing islands with houses and then roads, as the development of an imaginary town grew. I was, perhaps, seven or eight years old at the time. I could also work with watercolours and charcoal. When coming to live in Southampton, a nearby friend called Alan Fielding introduced me to oil paints. I established a small studio in the conservatory. You can see it behind my sister and me in Image 8. Dad painted the glass in its ceiling green in order to reduce the heat gain and make it more viable. I even pondered becoming an artist, whilst exploring the possibility of joining the Ordnance Survey, which was based in Southampton. When I learned of Architecture in my mid/late teens, as part of studying for my A Levels, I concluded that arena was where my future lay.

As I share more of my own journey at this still formative stage, I am sure you will be able to do the same. Your context will be different, as will be the route, but a journey it will have been. If you have not already, do write it down and do so even when there are tears among any joys.

For, as my own journey unfolded, I remember seeing another look on my dad's face. This time, it was the opposite of a 'cold chill'. Having been denied the opportunity of becoming a draughtsman, I saw his enjoyment that his past could now, in a sense, be fulfilled in my future. He did not say, but, whilst being pleased for me, I could sense that he was also quietly grateful that I could become, in effect, what he could not. As a result, I too was quietly pleased that my future could now be a form of fulfilment of his past.

Add that to my dad's dad being a joiner, working on the railways in Darlington, and there was also a legacy in craft and construction that could live on in my intended future. My granddad died soon after my training started. Whenever we visited, he used the word 'honey', in his warm northern accent, when referring to me. I knew that he was pleased that his life's work was to live on in me. Again, do have that in mind as we move ever nearer to the impact that is, for many, yet to register.

As you have seen, my architectural studies were to have as their point of reference emerging themes, focused on the questions I have raised here. Each was to help me prepare to serve my own clients as customers in the decades ahead. They were also a form of fulfilment for at least three generations in the life of my family: my own, my dad's and my granddad's. As a result, I was on a journey that was part of a flow of history that embraced far more than just me. As we continue forward through these pages, do feel able to compare notes in your own sequence of generations.

For, you may find that your life is also part of a flow of history, rooted in the lives of others. You may even find that you are fulfilling the longings of many generations before your own. You may then find that a sense of fulfilment may then be relevant to the deadly serious context coming toward us all. That notion will be explored more fully in due course.

Many of the lessons I have learned in my own life journey have been as practical as they have been mind, as well as heart, stretching. Crucially, they have also led to an answer to the core question that I have highlighted. It is an answer that, for me, makes sense of the many layers of history from which my life has grown. It is also an answer that can, I am sure, do the same in your own unique context. When that answer came, it was a climax in my process of spiralling-in and it came from a source that took me by surprise. In the years since, all the other related questions I had been asking then had a point of reference, with their own answers following.

As we continue to spiral-in toward my answer, allow me now to bring in another dimension that is directly relevant to our global predicament. It is that the dominant element on our home planet is water. For, water is as meaningful as it is practical. It enables life to live. Water can also kill and overwhelm even nations. It could also destroy our world.

That is why I started my Introduction and now this heading with a photograph of me by a river. I am with Jenny by a weir, with the highly pressured volume of water behind being the River Thames as it flows through Oxford.

One major strategy

As a taste of what lies ahead as we journey forward, in Image 14 is an illustrative drawing prepared by a former team member, Alistair Beckett. It is of a project that I have been developing for just over 20 years, with other colleagues now being involved. It is for a series of nine green energy generating inhabited bridges, with each linking the north and south banks of the River Thames. They are not to the west of London, as in Image 12. These substantial structures are all proposed for the east side of the capital from the City to the Thames Estuary. Their purpose, in addition to being much-needed river crossings, is to:

a. Harness the power of a mighty river in its tidal region as a green energy powerhouse, whilst at the same time:

b. Protecting the millions of people that would suffer if the present flood defences proved to be inadequate due to accelerating climate change and sea levels rising. As a result:

c. The goal is to work with negatives and turn them into positives. It is also:

d. To buy time for life on our home planet. When imagining London as a clock face, the proposal could transform an urban region from 1.30 to 4.30, with the River Thames passing through at 3.00. Its title is: A LONDON WATER CITY. I will explain more in due course.

It has taken some 20-plus years to reach the current stage and, due to my age, I may not see that strategy implemented. But, whilst I have some energy, having now planted a seed of a solution, I will continue to work and help it grow. You will see other examples in due course of equivalent projects. All are my response as we move toward a climax in our world's flow of history. It is to address the effects of climate change in a way that is as proactive as possible. As a result, my commitment is not to give up and not do anything. Indeed, it is the opposite.

The proposal in Image 14 is, therefore, an insight into what I think is needed to prepare a region to the east of central London for what is to come. I have also been asked to apply its principles to my former home city of Southampton. For, the Leader of its City Council sees my thinking as being directly relevant to the same issue he is facing. It is of climate change, with sea levels rising, so much so

Image 14: A green energy generating inhabited bridge for the East Thames

the city's existing flood defences could be overwhelmed. The danger, therefore, is that water could become a deadly enemy.

When responding to a request for help in Southampton, I was very aware that water had shaped the very identity of the communities that my parents served so well. The ships that traversed the seas then generated the employment so key to the well-being of their customers, as friends to my family. The place and the community where I learned about a sense of belonging was now endangered and seriously so.

Such belonging can be experienced when relationships are shared. It can also be felt very tangibly in places, such as a shop and in a street. It can infuse small gatherings of two or three, as well as ones much larger. It can be evident in shared activities and especially ones that are enjoyed. Scale seems not to be an impediment. For, watching a game of football in a stadium or listening to music in a concert hall are contexts where an ever larger, even dynamic, sense of belonging can be felt. Such a belonging can also be evident in a school, in a garden, a factory or an office. It can be experienced in a village, a town, a city, a county and in a national, as well as in a pan-national, context.

My goal is that it will be re-kindled, by adopting a strategic approach for Southampton and its several water frontages, modelled on the proposals in London. A fundamental goal is to work with the life enabling qualities of water and do so in a way that also respects its destructive capabilities. It is then to harness that power for shared good and enhancement for people in a place. The proposal could even enable the city's football and athletic club, 'the Saints', to extend its remit into water-borne activities of substance. More on this anon, for its implications are relevant to many other comparable and endangered situations around the islands of the United Kingdom and our world.

When thinking about 'the Saints', I first drafted these paragraphs in 2018. The Football World Cup was in full swing in Russia as an event that lasted over several weeks. Through it, we saw many local and national manifestations of strongly felt identities and belongings. There was, however, a constant danger that one belonging could challenge another. Some might have done so in negative ways that undermined a shared belonging. Nevertheless, when shared, that belonging had one focus, which was football.

Those positive feelings can be momentary when, for example, greeting a friend. They can also be focused on smaller events, such as celebrating a birthday or as a family entering a new year. A sense of belonging can even be evident in the words we use when talking with others. It can also be enabled by the way we approach, move around and through a place. What we then see and the way we see it can then contribute to the feeling that 'This is where I belong.'

All those contexts were in mind when the London Water City was conceived. All are then, once again, in mind when I explore how its principles could be applied, not just in Southampton, but also the Solent region. For, the same deadly issue of sea levels rising is there for Gosport, Portsmouth and the Isle of Wight, just as it does beyond. A total approach is, therefore, needed as we all respond to the prospect of a global end here on Earth.

Enabling belonging

Even our voices can be part of enabling an experience of a sense of belonging. That sense can inhabit the atmosphere of the accent of one region, which will vary from that of another. Being from the North East of England, I smile with enjoyment when hearing a Geordie twang, for I remember my mum. Her voice was then part of the sense of belonging enjoyed by my parents' customers in their shop, especially when in Southampton. In addition to an accent, tone can be key in the way we communicate one with another. The way we look and listen to a person can also either enable a belonging or can have the opposite effect. Hand gestures and body language, the same.

Around our world, people use many different spoken and written languages to communicate and share. Most people living in France will speak French and most of their neighbours in Germany will speak German. Many then learn each other's language in order to converse and share. Every rising generation also seems to invent new phrases that only they initially understand. Each becomes part of who they are becoming. Those words can then become common parlance.

The design of places then adds to those linguistic variations. Paris is identifiably different from London, with both being different to Rome. A town in southern Germany that I knew as a lad, Bad Tolz, shares similar market town characteristics with my new hometown of Witney, here in England. Yet, the design language that enables a sense of belonging in Bavaria is distinctly different to that here in West Oxfordshire.

As you may expect, when highlighting this range of languages and contexts, my question is:

. Why do they exist?

That question, as always, has then to be set in the context of the CHALLENGE facing us all. This is not least because we must communicate and debate, perhaps, as never before. The same question also applies to our deep need to express identities and belong.

. Why do we need to express our belonging?

For, it can lead to conflict, even when only in sport. Our shared global predicament must lead to working relationships as never before and not the opposite in adversity.

Different languages can be a barrier and, from there, a justification for separation, subjugation and even the domination of one group of people over another. That outcome will, I am sure, accelerate an end. As a result, a sense of belonging must rise through mutual respect and proactive debate.

Many have said that mutually supportive relationships are more likely when our global community can communicate. The implication being that, if we do not communicate the opposite can then happen. We may then cease to understand each other, only emphasising our own identity-based belongings and not those of others.

Yet, many are also realising that communication alone is not enough. There must be mutual respect and appreciation. There must also be a shared goal. In the context of the predicament we all now face, it can only be the well-being of our planetary home and all of its inhabitants.

Clearly, THE BIGGEST CHALLENGE must be understood. Debate requires communications and language, just as it requires insight and understanding. Of necessity, an agreed shared goal is crucial as are words that we can all grasp.

In the midst of so many languages, my goal is to highlight a further language that I have come to call 'the design language of life.' My view is that it can be a vehicle for communication and a themed point of reference. You will see what I mean by that in due course. For, the existence of so many languages must not deny the core need we all have. It is to face and respond positively to the predicament we now all face. It is to communicate, mutually understand and support each other, with the goal of enabling a shared global belonging with an Earth that enables life.

Names are important in the context of belonging. Mine was to be 'Raymond Hall'. My parents chose it in memory of my dad's brother, who was tragically killed at the Battle of El Alamein during World War Two. His loss was deeply felt, not least because he was always 'the life of the party'. Mum and dad then panicked, wanting me to grow to be me and not feel that I should be like him. They, therefore, added John as my first name and I became 'John Raymond Hall'. I was, nevertheless, always called Ray and have grown to adulthood as 'Ray Hall'.

There will be reasons why you are named as you are. Whatever your name, it identifies you as being 'you', just as mine does for me. Our names then enable both you and me to know who we are as unique people. Having identified that uniqueness, we can relate, communicate and potentially belong. We can also do so with other unique people, who also have names. As you have seen, I grew watching my mum and dad speak with customers. Remarkably, they always seemed to know their names.

As I write, the scale of the migrant crisis in the Middle East, North Africa and Central America points to a harsh reality. For many deeply painful reasons, it is a loss of belonging in many communities and in many places. The outcome is as painful as it is practical. It is homelessness. When seeing the pain felt by others, I am even more grateful for the sequence of places that I have known as homes. I have also been privileged to have lived in each fundamentally out of choice. My daughters have been able to do the same. Each place has then helped three generations of the Hall family to be who we are as individuals and as a shared 'as-one'.

As a result, just as I have a name, I also have an address. By having both, I know who I am and where I am privileged to live and belong. Anyone I meet can then learn of that identity and of that place-based belonging. In my youth, my home address happened to be the same as a shop, which, in turn, had a name. In Southampton, it was 'Merry Oak Stores' because of the area where we lived. As a shop, it belonged to two people, whose names were discreetly and openly displayed. They were 'J. and N. Hall', thereby telling of my mum and dad, 'Jessie and Norman Hall'. Their names and my name, the address of my home and the name of the shop were then all key to identifying and expressing many dimensions of a shared belonging.

It was a belonging that was felt by my family and my parents' customers. It was also one that they consciously helped engender in their community. That belonging deepened as my mum and dad got to know and use the names of their customers. One consequence was that customers also came to know each other. When I look back, I became aware that many knew each other in the street, but not by name. Mum and dad, in a sense, enabled superficial relationships to grow, with names being shared and known. As customers talked in the shop, those conversations would often continue outside. A sense of shared belonging then steadily became very visible. It initially had a focus in a shop, but then it grew to encompass other aspects of all our daily lives.

As I have mentioned, another consequence was that my sister and I were well known in our area, so much so that customers were not only friends, they were almost 'guardians' as part of our family. I felt safe as a result. There were also many occasions when I was helped by such a customer friend. Allow me to introduce you to one such 'family' member in the photograph in Image 15.

It was taken some 30 years ago. My dad had, by then, died. As part of a grieving process, my mum wanted to meet old friends in Southampton. She is with Rita Mini Dalrymple outside what had been 'Merry Oak Stores' in Sholing Road. Rita was a customer, who was part of our 'family' and we were part of hers. Her husband often helped me repair my motor scooter and later my first car, an old Mini. My daughters, Becs and Claire, are with them. I especially enjoy the way Rita Mini is holding their hands. They had not met before, but in a matter of minutes there was trust and friendship. Both of those qualities were there in my childhood and they could still be felt in the generation that followed. Belonging, therefore, is real and deep. It can also be long-lasting, with trust and care following.

Image 15: My mum with Rita, Claire and Becs

Allow me now to say a little more.

Memories

In the photograph, the recreation ground I walked across to go to school is in the distance. Rita lived across the road from the shop in a council house. Her husband was originally from the Caribbean. He was very mechanically minded, but his paid work was intermittent and he used his spare time helping people like me. Their son was an ace swimmer in the local pool. I watched him dive and learned. As a result, I grew wanting to emulate all three of those special people.

For, I loved Rita and I can hear her voice as I type, with tears rising.

As you can see from the photograph, my mum and Rita were as much a two-as-one on that visit as they were when we lived above the shop. I was especially pleased to introduce my daughters to her. In more recent times, following a business meeting in Southampton, I took the opportunity to call by. Rita had by then died as had her husband, with the shop now being a dance academy. Memories flooded back of an era past, as well as of years in between, and I was grateful.

For, shortly after I completed my courses in Architecture and Planning, dad became seriously ill with cancer and had to sell both the shop and our home. Mum was told that he had two years to live. They then left Southampton and moved back to Darlington, where they were able to reconnect with close friends from their younger days. Four years later, dad died on the couch of his home in Brinkburn Road. I was with him when that final moment came. He was almost skeletal, but he shone. His arms were skin and bone, yet he was able to raise them and I am sure I could hear voices welcoming him home.

Some four decades later, more tears rise even now when I remember that special time.

As you can see from the photograph of mum with Rita, the sense of belonging my parents helped engender in their community was felt long after their time in Southampton. That belonging remains part of my life and continues on as a form of legacy. I trust this inheritance will be valued by the generations that follow.

When at school there, I learned about Architecture. Thanks to a grant from its City Council, I gained a college place in London, as I prepared for my life's work. Fifty-plus years later, this son of Southampton may soon be able to help the city of his youth. It would be by making its people and place more ready to play their role as part of THE BIGGEST CHALLENGE, due to climate change and sea levels rising. If that happens, I would be both honoured and pleased.

A design language

All the clients I sought to serve in the decades since my student days have been real people living and working in real places, just like Rita Mini, but different. Each was as unique and as special as those in my parents' shop. Each had a name. Each also lived, worked and enjoyed their leisure time in a place of many places that would also have names. All those names were part of a language that told of the identity of people and where they had felt, in varying ways, at least a glimpse of a sense of belonging.

In order, therefore, to be as effective as possible, my focus became understanding how design could help enable that precious sense of belonging for people in a place.

I had, therefore, to understand with an ever-greater clarity what belonging was and how I could help it come into being. Words helped, but, thanks to my early college training, other ways of summarising ideas came within reach. Some were visual and required simple drawing skills. For me, they included a sequence of diagrams. Each then helped me define what I saw as being the core ingredients in a sense of belonging. An ever larger, but still outline, framework of ideas also began to emerge. So much so that I was soon able to test them in design practice. I will introduce you to several of those diagrams, as well as their consequences in the design of places shortly.

For now, do simply note that a process was coming into being. It was one of defining insights, using diagrams and words, and then testing each through specific schemes. That sequence then proved to be foundational to my approach to my subsequent work life. For, what emerged was not only a way of thinking about the design of buildings, it was also a way of seeing the world around and within me. From there, it was a way of understanding and relating to life itself.

In the decades which followed, that emerging world view, therefore, informed, not only my approach to the design of a wide variety of projects, it also informed my understanding of every dimension of life. That ever deepening and enlarging process had started with some observations and diagrams. Crucially, the themes summarised in those diagrams were then unexpectedly affirmed by a series of college exercises using – amazingly – ping pong balls. Again, I will give you an insight shortly.

For, they led to a specific as well as generic design. Although not built, it proved to be a crucial step towards an ever more clearly defined approach to the many client-based and constructed design projects that then followed. For, what in effect emerged was a design language, rooted in life and that I found to be very practical. Almost all those projects are in use today. As a result, the effect of that tentative student beginning is now visible in the lives of many people, as well as places.

In the pages that follow, you will see:

a. Some of those student diagrams. You will also:

b. Glimpse that design language and its huge implications. It was one that I discovered when assembling diagrams and clusters of those ping pong balls.

The first application of that language's principle was in the design of a generic building when at college. A very conspicuous and real-life community project in Brixton, in South London, then followed.

You will also see how that design language informed a wide variety of design projects, when serving clients in the several decades that followed. For, the scheme in Brixton led to me establishing a small multidisciplinary practice that, later, had associated offices around the UK and abroad. Along the way, I have been privileged to have worked with some very talented in-house teams, as well as many specialists in related disciplines and work arenas. Again, you will meet some as we journey forward.

When I introduce them to you, you will gain an insight into the role each played in schemes that were examples of theory applied in practice. You will also be able to assess whether an emerging way of seeing our world did, indeed, outwork into viable practice. When doing so, you may even find that you, too, feel the same sense of intrigue that I began to feel during those very formative years as a student and then a young design practitioner.

For, there was, indeed, something that was very intriguing about the diagrams and then the ping pong ball clusters that I assembled. That intrigue was because there were consistent geometries within each. Those geometries then seemed to inhabit every aspect, not only of my life, but also, I suspect, of yours. Indeed, I increasingly saw those geometries every day of my own life and in everybody's life. It was not long before they became apparent in the multiple dimensions of the life of our Earth and cosmos. If you find yourself seeing them as I did, you may also be as intrigued as I certainly became.

More on diagrams and ping pong balls anon in Heading Seven. For now, some further thoughts as preparation.

For, the context of that sense of intrigue was always the seeming contradiction between belonging and an end in life. One consequence was that, as the implications of each diagram and ping pong ball cluster became ever more relevant, my awareness of the enormity of our global predicament grew. As that occurred, so did the scale of THE CHALLENGE before me and before us all.

When I drew the diagrams, my goal was that:

a. They might inform the content of a design and, from there that:

b. They may benefit the lives of the people and the places I was soon to serve.

I saw each diagram, therefore, as an enabler and as a servant. I also began to see each as a window into something far more. Indeed, I began to see the whole of life in the same way. Each aspect exists as something that is specific. At the same time, each is also a window into something far more. There was, as a result, that rising sense of intrigue. For, I knew that the implications of that possibility could be as vast as they could be detailed, when seen in the context of the core question 'why?'

That growing sense of intrigue then caused me to wonder whether there was a lot more to discover in what was still but a fledgling, albeit emerging, understanding of life. I also began to wonder whether those implications could be theoretical and practical, not only in my life, but also in all of our lives. I even wondered whether there was a 'something intrinsic within life' that might help me resolve the conflict that I have highlighted concerning belonging and death.

I will say a lot more as we journey forward, but that sense of intrigue soon became tantalising. For, it was as if that 'something' had a presence to it that then became almost 'magnetic'. As will be seen, that sensation later had consequences that were totally unexpected. They were consequences that then enabled me to access, what I now deem to be trustworthy answers to the huge questions that I have asked. They are about life's very reason for being. They are answers that first require an even bigger picture.

Heading Five

BELONGING AND CONTEXT

Image 16: A cliff edge

Whenever I approach a cliff edge

Fear grips me and I step back

Yet other creatures fly beyond unafraid

They even seem to relish the opportunity

Why can they do that and not me?

Allow me now to briefly unpack something of my understanding of a phrase that has become ever present in these pages. It is 'a sense of belonging' and starts with:

'A SENSE OF'

Words can summarise, albeit often inadequately, the deepest emotions felt by human beings. An example is the one I have just highlighted. As a phrase within a phrase, 'a sense of' can point to an experience or insight that refers to the essence of its companion word. In this context, it is, 'belonging'. When doing so, it can also point to an underlying motivation, as well as even a form of driver, within and behind that focal word.

As I have suggested, another word can then seek to encapsulate that deeper reality. That word is 'love'. It hosts a meaning, about which a multitude of letters, poems, plays, films and music have been written. To know love, to be loved, to give and share love is a need that, I suspect, is there within all of us. Indeed, it is a need that has been there within, at least, human beings for millennia. The care shown by, say, swans, elephants and lions to their offspring may also suggest we are not alone amongst living beings.

As you have seen, that is why early in my own journey I concluded that enabling a sense of belonging could only occur if there is love for others. For me, that included my place of work. I had, therefore, to allow love to be my point of reference. Yet, when knowing of so many attempts to seek a definition of the meaning of the word 'love', I wondered whether doing the same would ultimately be impossible.

What I did know was that 'belonging' could be felt and even described, just as the effect of 'love' can be seen in the lives of people. I also knew that both could then be evident in the fabric of places. My own home was an example, alongside my mum and dad's corner shop. As a result, enabling a precious experience of belonging in a place could be an outworking of loving others. Logically, the sequence could then work in reverse, with enabling a sense of belonging being a prelude to love being experienced.

Even when recognising that a full definition of belonging and love may ultimately be out of reach, I concluded that both could be partially described. That then led to the diagrams that I have mentioned. As a result:

a. A journey began toward an ever-deepening understanding of belonging and, from there, why it is that we can know love. As I have shared, naively at first, I then applied those theoretical diagrams in design practice and did so when as a student. With lessons then learned, I continued that process through my workplace as an Architect. And:

b. From the outset, my goal of using emerging design skills to enable that ever deeper sense of belonging seemed to be one that, with caution and care, was realistic.

For, I had seen the relevance of belonging and love in the physical setting of my parents' workplace. In the now five decades since first drawing my diagrams and applying their implications in practice, the quiet confidence I felt then has not lessened. Indeed, it has grown, with the many pages set out here, as well as the other Steps that will follow, being a consequence.

Once again, you will be able to say if that confidence is justified, when glimpsing and learning more about the projects that I will show you. If in some small way, you do feel that I have enabled others to experience a sense of belonging and to feel loved, I would be pleased. If you do not, my goal would be to learn from any critique and move forward from there. As a result, the diagrams are me 'sensing' and seeking to describe what 'a sense of belonging' means as theory, with the goal of theory being applied in actual practice. That 'sensing' is, hence, not absolute. It was a starting point that might lead to more.

The word that completes that core phrase is then:

'BELONGING'

As I trust you will appreciate, early in my explorations, I became aware that trying to over-define an experience can have a negative effect. When pondering the meaning of words such as 'love' and 'belonging', expressed insights can grow, with each being helpful. Nevertheless, they can also cause something that is vibrant and warm, as well as almost fathomless and immeasurable, to become too contained. That can lead to an opposite feeling, which is a certain 'coldness'. When that happens, any experience of precious meanings can start to die.

As a result, I recognised the danger of sterilising the meaning of 'belonging', even when as an insight into the meaning of the word 'love'. For, I knew that there was the possibility of making their meanings an object, instead of a heartbeat. When you ponder the diagrams that I will show you under Heading Seven, do know that I was aware of that risk when first drawing them. I am also aware that I am taking a risk when showing them to you. For you may find them 'cold', even when they are not meant to be.

With that as a backcloth, allow me to attempt to define the core word 'belonging'.

For, rooted in the examples I have given, belonging is when two personal 'worlds' communicate and share. It is when one 'world', in a multitude of ways and depths, enters the 'life' of the other. It may be momentary. It may be long-lasting. It may be between individuals or it may be between groups of people, even nations. As a result, part of the life of one is enjoined with part of the life of the other.

That process had occurred in a deep and long-lasting way for my parents as Jessie and as Norman. So much so that they became as one in marriage, with a shared name following: that of 'Hall'. Throughout, the reason for that belonging had been love. The love they shared had been both the motivator and the driver of their shared belonging.

That belonging then embraced my sister, Barbara and me, just as it touched the customers they served through their corner shop. When you look at my diagrams, do picture each of the people I have highlighted. For, each will be represented as a unique circle, with each circle then having a name. As one circle relates to another, with each becoming part of the other's life, do then imagine the resultant relationships as circles overlapping in many, as well as different, ways. When that happens, the outcome can always be the same. It can be a shared sense of belonging. At whatever variance in depth, that belonging can be felt.

I have mentioned the quiet confidence that I felt as I started this exploratory process as a student. I was certain there was theory within life that I had not understood and that I could understand. My expectation then was that it could help me design what I began to call 'people places'. The generic scheme at college, as emerging theory applied, was then called 'a Meeting Place'. An opportunity came in Brixton to apply its implications in practice. The outcome was a built scheme that was substantial and even acclaimed. It was also timely in what had become a multi-faceted and special, inner city community. I will say a lot more in Step Two.

An important dimension to note now is that, when still at college, the seed of the beginning of my life's work was sown. That seed grew to be a sapling in Brixton, with many other trees following as I explored in greater depth emerging theory applied in practice. That journey was also one of exploring what became my growing understanding of life's reason why.

When I look back, I am, as a result, grateful for the privilege of having been a student. I am also grateful for the approach adopted by the college where I studied. If you are a student, do, therefore, grasp the opportunity before you and do so knowing that your own journey may now be able to gain a seed-like focus. It may even be that you will find that you can love others through your own future workplace. If that is the outcome, as one member of the broader community, I would be pleased and grateful. For, even if we never meet, my life will have been touched by yours for good. It may also be that you will then feel the same sense of intrigue that I felt, with a sense of a 'magnet' quietly being there.

Having shared that, I am aware that I have just used the phrase 'for good', with a special focal word, which is 'good'. It is a word that also needs defining. More on that anon too, therefore. For, it is crucial.

When I look back from my 73rd year, I am amazed that, in the many decades since my early student days, insights have led to an ever-enlarging theory about life. The insights gained have also been applied in some 400, very varied design contexts and at different scales. They have been for the many clients I and my teams have been privileged to serve. They have also directly informed the several development strategies that I am exploring, including the 'Water Cities', as well as many other initiatives that I have been pleased to pursue.

They have all come into being by being, what I have come to call, 'brass rubbed into existence'. As we journey forward, alongside 'belonging', 'love' and 'good', do note that phrase 'brass rubbed into existence'. For, it too is fundamental to my understanding of life's reason for being, even when in the context of death.

With each project more insights came. Their focus was the design of places for people. The practice I formed in 1972 came into being when I was still at college. It was initially called 'Raymond Hall Design Services'. That was because I could not initially use the term 'Architects'. It is protected by the Architects Registration Board and I had not completed my full training. As a result, I had to work with practitioners who were already qualified. I could only do that by employing fully qualified Architects, who were far more capable than me. When I had worked under each for the necessary hours and passed a theory-into-actual practice exam, I changed the name to 'Raymond Hall Architects'. My declared goal throughout was consistently to enable an ever-deeper sense of belonging for people in places.

The office brochure sheet in Image 17 tells of that commitment, with some of the schemes that were examples of theory, by then, being outworked in practice. There you will see in model form a number of those schemes, with each held by people dear to me. Some were from within my steadily growing office. Others were friends from outside. My wife, Jenny, is at the top and our daughter, Becs, is there as a babe bottom left. She is the only part of the gathering that was added after the event. Her photograph was taken on a family holiday near Newquay. It was when she was enjoying the taste of her first pebble. My mum is halfway down on the right-hand side and was a crucial team member, as a specialist in tea and toast.

Unusual for me, I am wearing a dickie bow. Others include a good friend of my mum, as well as close friends of mine, Asouguo Ebong, a former tribal chief from Nigeria, married to Kitura from Jamaica. Their two children, Elizabeth and Joseph, are also there. Do then note the man on the right holding an architectural model. His name is Graham Stevensen, which ends in 'sen' and not 'son'. He is proud of that distinction. You will read more about Graham as we journey forward. He was an Associate in my office at the time and became the project Architect for several early schemes, as a very skilled practitioner. To his right are his former wife and their two children, Matthew and Andrew, who are in yellow.

Do then note the mission statement. It is that of enabling 'a sense of belonging' for people in places.

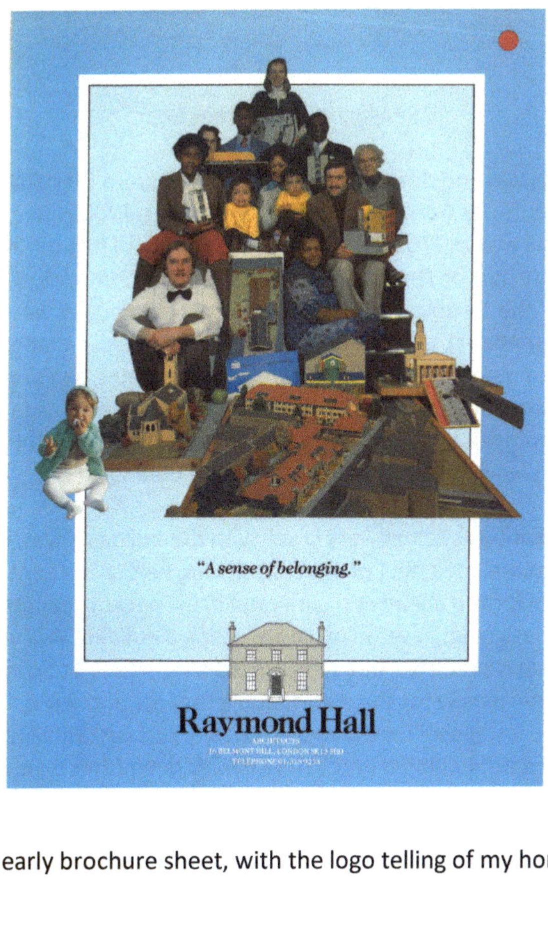

Image 17: An early brochure sheet, with the logo telling of my home and office

As soon as that precious experience was evident through a range of completed projects, I concluded to rename the practice, 'People and Places Architects'. I also changed the logo from being the house, where Jenny and I lived above my office. It then became one that told of people and of places, with each belonging in a relationship together as one. I will tell you more about that logo shortly. For now, it is in Image 18.

PEOPLE AND PLACES

International

www.raymondhall.co.uk

Image 18: My current logo

Several other design and development-based companies then followed that embraced Interior Design, Graphics, Landscapes, Project and Cost Management, as well as Property Consultancy work. All had different names and were initially part of The Raymond Hall Group of Companies. Each then became part of the 'People and Places Group'. One company was 'People and Places International' as a vehicle for shaping strategies that could involve contexts beyond our shores. For, associations were being explored with other practices that would enable an almost global reach. As we journey forward, you will also meet some of the special people that were involved. Their focus, in varying degrees, was that of 'enabling a sense of belonging'.

Marketplace downturns can be very cruel, with the building investment world tending to feel the effect of a recession long before the general public. For, clients often looked ahead and understandably became cautious before committing to designing, never mind constructing a building. As I write, a global recession of scale is predicted due to the lockdowns needed to combat the Coronavirus. I feel deeply for the many people that are and will be affected. For, even though the last global recession did not fully surface until 2008, I was by then carrying the accumulated debts from earlier downturns. With other factors, including some wrong decisions on my part, it meant that each 'People and Places' company became vulnerable. One by one they had to close, with 'People and Places Architects Ltd' being the last to go into voluntary liquidation in March 2007. Only the non-trading 'People and Places International Ltd' survived.

The sense of grief that I felt was profound, especially when redundancies were necessary for people who meant a lot to me. Other arrangements had also to be made for clients I was still serving. It was a very painful end to what had been 'a vision' that had become a living and working reality for more than 30 years, even if only then as a glimpse of what might have been possible.

The sense of failure and loss that I also felt was acute. For, so much effort by so many people had seemingly come to naught. If anyone reading these pages has been directly involved in or is being affected by such an experience, I know how it feels. The pain goes very deep and the effect is bewildering. Like 'love' and 'belonging', those feelings cannot ultimately be defined, nor can they be fully contained in words. Nevertheless, each can be felt because both are real.

As with a broken personal relationship or the loss of someone dear due to illness, I have since sought to understand and then express what I was feeling. I did so in another diagram, telling of breakdown, that you will see in Heading Seven. For, that experience helped me explore more fully the 'dying' dimension of the huge questions that I am exploring here. There was a sense in which, starting in my student days, a new future had become a reality. 34 years later in 2007, when 'People and Places Architects Ltd' closed, that future had seemingly come 'crashing to the ground'.

It was the strain of trying to avoid that demise that led to my health failing. Aged 59, my own end then seemed to be in prospect. I was in my office reception talking with my PA, Kam, when all I could do was fall back and sit in a chair. I knew something was very wrong. The only words I could say were, 'Please get Jenny'.

Tears have come as I have shared aspects of this journey with you. I did not expect them to rise now, but they have as I typed those words. Perhaps, it was the sense of grief that I felt. Perhaps it was remembering terrific people I had worked with, as well as the places we had all helped bring into being. Perhaps it was also being aware of my vulnerability, knowing there was nothing more that I could do, other than asking for Jenny.

My lady did come and helped me home. For quite a while, I was almost unable to move. All I could manage was to simply lie on my bed. There was an initial misdiagnosis of the problem, which was followed by panic. That came when it was realised that my thyroid had almost stopped functioning. I was immediately placed on a regime of thyroxine, as a substitute. I then realised, even more precisely, how each part of my body, including a small gland, is needed to enable me not just to live an effective life. It was to live at all. You may have had an equivalent experience, or know someone who has, with the same conclusion coming to the fore. For me, it was a very sobering realisation.

It took a long time to recover and it was a slow process. Gradually I was then able to look to the future with some expectation, albeit still with limited energy and no office as back-up. In parallel, it took my accountant and good friend, Peter Willans, some two-plus years to resolve the many professional and financial issues caused by my practice's closure. One consequence was that I was not now responsible as an employer for the well-being of others. I will be quite open with you and say that it was a huge relief.

As a result, I could refocus my thinking and activities and could do so as my energy steadily revived. A new era was dawning that had a renewed sense of clarity. That era was now in the context of a deepened certainty concerning my own limitations and vulnerability, as well as very specifically my mortality. For, I could have died.

As I have mentioned, the only company to survive was one that had not traded. Its purpose was as a vehicle for shaping major development strategies. It also held the intellectual property of several projects, including a number of strategies that I had initiated. One was the proposal that I have mentioned for a series of green energy generating, inhabited, flood defence bridges, as in Image 14. That company was called 'People and Places International'. I still use it today. For, it too has the same goal of enabling a sense of belonging, but this time in the larger context of strategic approaches to resolving problems in urban and other contexts.

I have, therefore, used that vehicle when exploring strategies that were not architectural or planning focused, but which nevertheless could help communities of varying scales. They included whole nations, as well as even our world. You will see examples of each as we journey forward. Whatever the context, my goal has always been the same. It is to enable the maximum positivity for individuals and groups of people in the place where they live, work and enjoy their leisure time. It is to do so whilst there is time, due to our global predicament.

Despite our negative context, that positivity has, at its heart, the goal of enabling a sense of multi-dimensional belonging. It is a belonging that, in turn, can provide a context for what I came to call, not just 'love', but 'selfless love'.

That further context was now with a deeper understanding of the reality we all face personally concerning our own mortality. Tragically, it was also with the evidence-based expectation that there is a time limit on viable life here on this our Earth.

Not running an office provided time to explore more fully that context. It included an emerging understanding of a world view that embraced an equally multi-dimensional, but nevertheless highly focused, answer to the question 'why?' As I have shared, this book is one direct consequence. It had been brewing throughout my student and working life, but I had not had the opportunity to consolidate a lifetime of thinking applied in practice. As you will realise, I did not ask my thyroid if it would almost cease functioning, in order to provide such an opportunity, but in retrospect I am grateful that it did.

As I entered my 60s, that opportunity came, therefore, in an unexpected way. In my latter years, I have been able to harness the journey of a lifetime. That context has, therefore, been helpful. Facing the prospect of my own end has also been relevant to our journey together now. There may be other occasions when I will need medical help. Whatever happens, I know my life will still come to an end, just as it will for all of us.

As I trust will have become evident, through these pages, my goal is to give insight on the many lessons that I have learned over 70-plus years. I am doing so in ways that are personal and social, physical and emotional, as well as local and globally based. I will also be setting each in a flow of history that has a beginning and is moving toward an end. As part of that ever-bigger picture, all those insights are evidence-based. They embrace frameworks of governance that are statutory, charitable and even political. All these dimensions are then relevant to the fact that people need viable places in which to live, even when knowing that life is in the context of death.

Architecture

As part of a spiralling-in process, allow me now to say a little more about Architecture.

For, a place is often a building, which in turn needs a piece of land where it can be built. Land must be bought, requiring the involvement of specialists in legal matters. The design of a building must, almost always, be approved by Planning authorities, requiring policy frameworks and the expertise of statutory bodies and politicians. Contractors are needed to build a building, with management skills and technical training needed. Materials have then to be sourced and made available, with all the resource and marketing opportunities each engenders.

Without a place, a design is merely an idea that cannot be used in practice. As an idea it cannot even be fully tested. It might inspire, but it will not enable the depth of belonging for others that has been my life's goal. Ideas might help change thinking, but the degree of change now needed in response to our global predicament, requires visible action, as theory that has practical consequences.

A building, when designed and built, can enable people to belong positively in a place. I have seen that happen on multiple occasions. It can then be evidence that any theory behind its design has worked in, what I came to call, 'nitty gritty' practice. As a result, the purpose of that building must be relevant to and supportive of its occupants, living in a place.

Crucially, that building has also to be relevant to the world around us all. That principle also applies, not just when it is in use, but also over time. That is why many of the photographs of projects you are seeing were taken following years of use and hence occupation, with their effect being evident in practice. It is only then that it is possible to see whether each has been a positive contribution to a world view, as an insight into the answer to the question why.

For a home, an office or a gym – and, indeed, any building – must have a purpose that is context based, as well as context focused. Both the purpose and the context must be as immediate and local, as they must be regional, national, global and even cosmic. It is a purpose and a context that have also to be relevant to a journey back in time, just as they must be relevant to a journey forward in time into the future. Thinking that embraces all those dimensions must be understood, as well as described, before a design can be seen to have any consistent validity, in terms of construction and effectiveness in use. That description can then provide a context for the seed of a design idea to be conceived. The work arena I have been occupying is, as a result, very much about context. It is about theory focused on context, applied in viable practice.

It is also an arena that is deadly serious, for, when buildings do fail, they can collapse and hurt, even kill, those within and around. As a result, theories and their application require rigorous testing in order to maximise the prospect of a positive outcome. Safety, viability and relevance in use cannot be assumed, nor do they just happen. With that sense of discipline in mind, as we journey forward, do be aware that the ideas, insights and experience I am sharing through these pages are rooted in a lifetime of such rigour, frequently applied. My own life's work is, as a result, anchored firmly in testing, as well as lessons learned over generations. That testing specifically applies in the statutory sector, where, as an example, the Great Fire of London in 1666 led to Building Regulations in use today that were painfully wrought.

In the UK, rigorous testing is applied in order to minimise the risk of failure and to maximise the prospect of viability. As a result, almost every new building requires a range of statutory approvals. They will only be granted if the scheme meets nationally, as well as locally based, regulations, rules and guidelines. Those design criteria are often embedded in law and administered through the governance of politicians, elected at local, regional and national levels. Even directives from the United Nations can apply, for example, concerning a site or context that has World Heritage status. The layering of regulation and control can, therefore, be legion. All have the goal of minimising risk to well-being and life, as well as maximising the opportunity for positive outcomes.

Relevantly all are a response to the conflicting context that I have highlighted of a desire to belong, when set in the context of the prospect of pain and of death. Do hold that in mind, as we seek to minimise the risk to life here on an endangered Earth, whilst also maximising the opportunities for positive outcomes.

Add to that layering of statutory oversight, one other dimension that is relevant. It is the fact that almost every scheme that I have been involved in will be seen almost every day. For, each will be seen by my clients, as well as their family, their friends and an unknown number of neighbours. It with those contexts in mind that the very tight and tangible constraints, within which I have been working over decades, will start to become apparent.

Anyone trying to suggest that those realities can be ignored would be foolish. For, to not recognise and honour the positive legacy from pain experienced over generations would be as disrespectful as it would be dangerous. It is that legacy, often enshrined in law, that has helped design practitioners like me be able to help clients establish a way forward in their lives, with the goal of the resultant scheme being as safe as is possible.

Understanding and responding positively and proactively to people in a place and in time is, therefore, fundamental for me as a designer. Just as it is, for me, as the person writing these pages, with my context being the predicament we all now face.

When affirming that, I am highlighting the need to generate positive outcomes from the far-reaching constraint of a deadly context. It is with the goal of being relevant to the context that we are all having to face. It is of an Earth that is in serious trouble and that may now be on its way toward a form of final collapse. For, our response to that biggest-ever constraint, as with the design of a building, will inevitably be a consequence of a very practical, as well as realistic, way of seeing our world.

It is a world:

a. Within which each one of us is living and that:

b. Is the life sustaining context that enables each one of us to live, to relate, to belong and even to love others and to feel love in return.

It is also a world that many are saying is dying. It is then a world that is still wonderfully alive and will remain so, whilst there is time. As a result, it is a world that:

c. Needs painful lessons learned over millennia harnessed to help us minimise risk and maximise opportunities where we can live, love and belong.

The world view adopted to ensure such positivity has to be by the many people and institutions affected, with each playing a crucial role. In that context, none of us are exempt. All of us are, in a sense, 'Architects' and 'builders', just as we are 'clients'. That is why it is vital that we all test any proposal that I, or anyone else, makes in response to the predicament we all now face. That principle applies as much to a building project, as it does to a regional strategy. Just as it also applies to any proposal even for national and global governance. More even than that, it applies to every arena in life, no matter who we are and where we are on this our endangered planetary home.

Each person inhabiting our Earth and those many layers of context will, in varying degrees, have to engage with that predicament. Across the UK as an example, at a local, regional and national level, many individuals and amenity groups are well able to take part in a process that has to lead to decision making, with action following. They can do so even before statutory approvals are sought, never mind granted. Indeed, it is not 'they', but 'we' who must do so. For myself and for the sake of the clients I have served, I have welcomed that challenge and discipline, even when it was not required formally.

Do also hold that thought in mind as part of an ever-bigger picture as we journey forward. For, such involvement, participation and engagement have to be our response to THE BIGGEST CHALLENGE as a result of the future coming toward each one of us. It is a future that we must face together. That is because we are all in life together, with my thoughts and world view actions affecting yours and vice versa. All must be tested, with what minimises the negatives and maximises the positives being the very necessary outcome. Those consequences can be consolidated in regulations and guidance, with a beneficial ripple effect that can accumulate to embrace everyone everywhere.

Allow me now to highlight another dimension rooted in my own arena of designing buildings.

Many people find it helpful to understand why, say an existing house, was designed as it was. When taking occupation, the insights gained would then enable them to anticipate how they would use it on a day to day basis. For, they were, in effect, to occupy a place that had already been designed and built as 'clothes' that were personal to the previous owners. To understand their reasons why for the design could then provide a context for the new occupants to define a new future in that place. As clothes, that place was about to become part of their lives. As a result, the inherited design will either enable, hold back, or even disable, the way they were to live their lives. In order to enable a positive response, an understanding of why from the past is needed. The occupant can then define how to bring into being a new future.

Apply that principle to the need for a new future on an endangered Earth. It then reinforces the need to understand how we have come to be in the situation we all now find ourselves as the current occupiers of our planetary home. My goal here is to do that, so that we can then plan forward with the maximum positivity.

As I trust can be seen, there are many dimensions to the relationship between people and places, just as there are many contexts relevant to the word 'belonging'. All apply as part of an outworking of the practical care inherent in 'love'. All are then directly relevant to our quest here, as I seek to help us to prepare for what is coming.

A context and a brief

A key point to affirm now is that the themes I am exploring are not just ideas. Each has very practical outcomes. They are, therefore, able and must be tested by many people in ever more detailed, as well as enlarging, contexts. Even if you live in Scotland, when one scheme is in London, its ripple effect will touch you. You may not be aware of that touch, but it will be there. It may also be that the thinking inherent in a scheme in London may be helpful 'north of the border', as well as elsewhere. As an example, I am certain that is the case with the green energy generating inhabited bridges in a London, or even a Southampton, Water City.

Similarly, if you live in Singapore or Cape Town, my actions will affect yours, just as your ideas will affect mine. That principle applies at both large and small levels. It is literally universal. There is then a sense in which our shared global predicament exists because of a lack of appreciation of that simple fact of life.

For me, therefore, all the projects I am showing you have been about a way of seeing and understanding our world. They are about what I have come to call:

THE DESIGN RELATIONSHIP BETWEEN PEOPLE AND PLACES

It is a design relationship that applies individually as well as globally for people in a place that is within many places. As you will see, all those places are then set in a local, regional, national, global, as well as even a cosmic, context. It is then a context of people and places in a flow of history and a framework that is time. It is a context infused by a desire to belong and a deeply felt need to love and be loved, despite the biggest constraint of all.

As I came to realise this, my need to understand accelerated, not just the reason for that constraint, but also for the biggest context of all. It is the reason why for life itself. That need was then helped by another parallel in my workplace.

For, as I have suggested, the design of every building starts with a reason why in the form of a 'brief'. That brief may be simply, 'to provide shelter for cattle when it is raining', summarised in as many words. It could then be expanded to include, 'whilst allowing the sun's warmth to be felt, with driving rain excluded'. Another phrase could also be added, such as, 'to enable the farmer, as well as the cattle, to get in and out easily'. More and more amplifications can then be forthcoming in a brief-forming process.

I trust you can imagine briefs for complex buildings, such as a hospital, being almost encyclopaedic in size. At whatever scale and whatever complexity, every building must have a reason why. With that in mind, do then see our Earth and its cosmos, not just as clothes or even as a home, but also as a mega building. It is one that already exists and did so before we were born. Like the house I have mentioned with new occupants, it too has a reason why. It was, let me use words from my own profession, 'designed and constructed' with a reason why. So much so that, for example, cattle can be warmed, whilst wind brought nourishing rain that enabled grass as their food source to grow. As a result, the whole of life could live.

Two key questions then became:

. What was the brief for our Earth? As a result:

. What is life's reason why?

If my analogy in Architecture has merit, that brief is the reason why that has led to the mega building that is our planetary home, set within its own cosmic context. That brief has, in turn, led to the specific shape of life as a design and a piece of construction. It is a place that has been occupied by human beings and an awesome array of living beings on land, in water and in the air. That brief and the nature of that occupation has then led to the condition of our Earth now, with the prospect of a form of structural collapse coming toward us all.

Such a notion has huge implications. For, if it is valid, I have come to realise that it challenges an equally huge range of assumptions that underpin and permeate much world view thinking in our modern era. I will say a lot more as we journey forward. As a taste now, my view is that those ways of seeing our world must be part of THE BIGGEST CHALLENGE and, from there, THE BIG DEBATE that I am advocating. Just as my own thinking must be tested, so must the thinking that is already out there.

Even if we may not realise its daily impact, its world view theory must be also exposed and tested based on outcomes in practice. That is, if we are to reach conclusions that can help our predicament be less so, by being theory that positively addresses the nightmare coming toward us. This is especially when knowing that the amount of time available is shrinking by the day.

I will not say any more at this stage. Much more will follow. My goal now is simply to sow the seed of an ever-bigger context for deeper exploration as we journey forward, Step by Step. In the meantime, I trust you can see why my journey led me to be intrigued about every dimension of life, no matter how small and how big, as well as no matter when or where.

An added dimension of intrigue was then another 'sense' that began to rise. It too may seem obvious, but for me it was tantalisingly so.

In the early years following the losses in 2007, my workplace team had to be just me, albeit with nearby colleagues and distant associates that I can call on. My workplace was not now an office, but my study in my home, which was then in southeast London. It is now in, what I call, my 'Man Cave', as a largish room in the roof of my subsequent home here in Witney that has that name on its door.

I have a basic music system and I am currently listening to a compilation of music, which was a gift from Jenny. It is by Hank Marvin, who in earlier eras was the lead guitarist with The Shadows. As a result, as I type, it is relatively easy for me to go down 'Memory Lane' and re-enter the past realms I am exploring here that may otherwise have been lost. You may have 'oldies' in your own music collection that might help you do the same. Memory Lane hosts joys, just as it hosts tears.

One further consequence of the demise of my architectural practice in 2007 was that I had to live without an income. That had been the case for several months before closure came. Staff members did not know, but it was necessary as I sought to keep 'our ship afloat'. As a result, the harsh reality that had affected so many of my mum and dad's customers, when a ship did not come in, impacted me and it did so 'big time'. For Jenny and me, it meant an ever-larger accumulated debt.

There had been several other times of hardship throughout the 34 years I had run a design practice, but I had always been able to move out of difficulties by generating an income. That was now not possible. My former practice, 'People and Places Architects Ltd', was not now an asset that could be sold. Indeed, it was the opposite. It was a very heavy liability. Having guaranteed its borrowings, I had to personally honour those commitments, which were six figures in size. The consequence, inevitably, was that Jenny and I had to sell our greatly loved home of 38 years to generate the funds needed. It was the home where my family and I had felt a deep sense of belonging.

You have seen a logo for 'Raymond Hall Architects' that summarised its design. I will show you some photographs as we journey forward. When you see them, I think you will understand why it was a place where we could belong, as well as be of help to others. For, it was a people place.

In amongst the pain of loss, however, there came a new context for a new era. It was akin to a gift that could be unwrapped. It was where I could, essentially unhindered, write down some of the many lessons I had learned. It was also a context where other people could test, as well as challenge with rigour, the theory into practice conclusions I had reached. Once again, I would recommend that scenario to anyone reading this, albeit with a much less painful way of enabling it.

As a specific, that context became the programme administered by Middlesex University (MU) towards what is called a 'Professional Doctorate by Public Works'. As the title implies, it was not only about theory, but also about its application in practice. It was, therefore, about evidence in the public arena that could be seen, described and challenged. I learned of it through an academic research institute in Oxford, for which MU was the validating body. If participating in the programme led to a positive outcome, my goals were then specific. They were:

a. To use whatever time remained in my now lengthening life in a way that was as positive as possible. It was then:

b. To make accessible any credible theory that outworked in practice and:

c. To do so, trusting it may be of help to as many people as possible. You are now reading one pivotal outcome as a means of doing so. It was also:

d. To then make a contribution to THE BIG DEBATE in response to THE BIGGEST CHALLENGE ever to face humanity by:

e. Openly sharing my life's journey and doing so with the benefit of knowing that my own end was coming ever closer. It would also be to do so as:

f. A gift from me to you.

A Professional Doctorate programme is relatively new and may not be known to many. Allow me to, therefore, say a little more about it now, as you may find it helpful, as well as relevant to your own situation. Its core goal is as simple as it is profound. It is to see the whole of our lives as being of value to others. Our lives are, as a result, an asset to be researched, with key lessons extracted and shared in a disciplined context of challenge and testing. That principle especially applied in a workplace arena.

Image 19: An insulating porch for two elderly ladies

By examining and articulating a lifetime of theory applied in working practice, the goal is then that an asset, perhaps hidden, will be seen and used by others. For all of us, that principle applies to our early educational and contextual beginning. It also applies – and perhaps far more so – as we all approach life's end. My own life span is now quite long. That longevity has given me many opportunities to outwork theory. Some have happened relatively quickly. The design and construction process can be lengthy, so 'relatively quickly' means a matter of months. Others have taken years and even decades to come to fruition. Many are still a work in progress.

As a result, the projects I have chosen as illustrations of my own emerging world view reflect that variation and are wide ranging. They include something small and something large, with the first being a porch for two elderly ladies, who were feeling draughts. One can be seen outside in Image 19.

Another is a development strategy for an urban region that complements the London Water City that has, so far, taken almost 25 years to reach a point of possible implementation. It has as its focus one substantial building that seeks to harness the positives from the past as we move into a vulnerable new future. It is a project that will directly affect the lives of, perhaps, everyone living in South London. It could also become world renowned.

For the proposal is for 'A New Eco Crystal Palace' and can be glimpsed in Image 20. It is to be a showcase for management systems and technologies that could enable our planetary home to live for as long as is possible. It would be constructed using photovoltaic steel and glass, with in-built ground and air source energy capture systems, as well as cooling using grey water. It could be a focal venue for a globally focused BIG DEBATE as a practical response to THE BIGGEST CHALLENGE now before us all.

Image 20: A New Eco Crystal Palace

I will say more about both the porch and the New Eco Crystal Palace as we journey forward. I will also highlight other projects and proposals, including some here in West Oxfordshire, where I now live. Along the way, you will see how very practical can be enabling our shared past to come alive in our present. That two-as-one asset can then help us to prepare for a deadly serious future that, in turn, brings opportunities 'for good'. All those schemes and proposals are about belonging for people in a place in time. All are also, crucially, a response to the biggest predicament we have ever faced here on our Earth.

None of the commissioned schemes would have come into being if I had not had a client, who was seeking help and willing to pay for the work to be carried out. Each design exists, therefore, because those clients existed. The same principle applies to the teams working with me. For every scheme required the input of others, who were more skilled in their specialist arenas than me. Those capabilities were in, for example, realms of technology, contractual management as well as computer generated drawing. Once again, you will meet some of them as we journey forward.

As a detail now, I prepared the several non-commissioned proposals simply because I thought they may be of help in the deadly serious context we all find ourselves. Do, therefore, see each proposal as a contribution from an involved observer and a fellow human being. That same principle also applies to other projects that you will not see. They are out there, with ripple effects already rippling. Each was set in the context of both the predicament we now all face and the need for practical answers to many questions why.

You will have your own versions of a design project or a strategy in your work arena. If you felt able to share each, as your own gift to our world, that would be special. If you have already done so, do know of my genuine gratitude through these pages.

For me, all my schemes and proposals point to a total approach. It is one that could grow even more by being tested, corrected and amplified. If that approach, following rigorous examination, is still seen to be in some measure credible, its themes could be adopted in other contexts. They could be locally based, as well as nationally and even internationally focused. If that was the case, it just may be that they may help more and more communities respond to the harsh realities we all now have to face. As I have mentioned, those local and global dimensions have led me to table strategic approaches to the way we are governed here in the UK. That, in turn, led to other proposals for the role our nation here in the UK could team-play on the world stage, as the impact of what lies ahead increasingly registers.

As a result of this ever-bigger picture, each design scheme and each strategy is an example of theory applied in practice at varying scales. Each is different and set in complementary contexts. Each is also a response to what I see as being an ultimate context. It is of a planet that hosts belongings in abundance but yearning for more, with so much having been lost. It is of a planet that is, it would seem, also dying. For me, therefore, even a porch is part of my response to the conclusion that I reached when as a student. It was then affirmed as we entered 'The Last Millennium' of viable life here on Earth.

Responsibility and accountability

As you will appreciate, the disciplines of Architecture, Planning, Interior Design and Development can lead to construction projects, with each being very visual in their different contexts. When referring to a Professional Doctorate program, they are 'public works' that can be seen every day. What cannot be seen is the often long and detailed briefing, design development, planning and regulatory processes that led to those practical outcomes.

The same principle applies to the major development strategies that are yet to become building projects. Whatever the scale, all those formative processes contribute to the reason why the end scheme is as it is. Once again, that process and outcome are part of the ever-bigger context I have pointed to that is people, place and time based. They are, as a result, integral within our shared Earth based, as well as cosmic, flow of history. All are constantly intertwined. None are, when remembering Paul Simon's song, 'an island'.

As a relevant aside, I was recently involved in a discussion with friends and colleagues I have known since my twenties. We were debating the origins of Donald Trump's approach to his role as President of the United States. As I trust will be evident, the themes explored could apply to anyone in any form of leadership. Indeed, they are relevant to us all.

One view was that his thinking is the consequence of a changed perception of our world, especially by many of his fellow citizens. Their thinking, in turn, was in the context of a bigger flow of history, with changing world views that have varied over centuries. In that context, President Trump's approach is a consequence of that much bigger, external process. His actions were then as a result of a form of world view conditioning, over which he had no influence. It was already there shaping everything he thought and did. Another view was that his approach is a consequence of an internal process. It was something within his control. As a result, he was fully responsible, as well as accountable, for the way he thought and acted. They are the consequence of his own internal processes, decision-making and actions.

One direct implication of the first process-related outcome was non-liability, as the thoughts stated and the actions taken were, in a sense, inevitable and not the advocate's responsibility. In a sense, it was 'society' and a larger flow of history that was the cause. The direct implication of the second was different. It was that Donald Trump was fully responsible.

My own view was that his approach is both the consequence of long and complex processes, as well as one that is his specific responsibility. The same principle then applies to me and to all of us. That is especially so when the actions we now take affect not even a whole nation, such as the USA, but the whole world as it approaches what appears to be the prospect of an end.

My reason for highlighting that is because we all have, what some call, 'free-will'. As a result, we can think independently, albeit always in the context of already existent world views. As a result, we can define and advocate our own thoughts, as well as respond to those of others. The way we respond will then lead to further consequences. We are all, therefore, responders to contexts and contributors who vary that context. The implication then is that we can all vary the world view that has led to the predicament we all now face. The further implication is that we can all learn how to think and act in a way that minimises negatives and maximises positives. If that happens, we may then be able to 'buy more time' and delay an end.

No one is outside of such an influencing context. Nor is anyone exempt from responsibility when playing a role in shaping a world view that helps us all help each other. For, none of us is 'an island'. We all need each other and so does the planet that sustains us. We are all always individuals and a collective at the same time – and we can be both with a goal: that of enabling life to live.

As a result, we all carry responsibility, so much so that we are all accountable for what is happening to every living being individually and globally. I will come back to this theme more fully in due course. For now, do simply note that its implications are not only huge, they are also directly relevant to our journey through these pages.

As a taste, there are currently people blaming others for the fact that our Earth is in trouble. Whilst I understand why they are doing that, my view, however, is that the much bigger and more accurate picture is more complex and deeply rooted than that. For, every one that has ever lived is accountable, which includes me alive today. Just as everyone who will live will also find themselves contributing in some way to the demise of our Earth as well. No matter how hard we try not to be, we human beings are a fundamental part of the problem. We are on a daily and an individual basis. By being social and relational, we then compound the problem, whilst at the same time being able to do the opposite.

When facing that seeming fact of life, I then gradually began to realise the issue goes even deeper and broader than that.

A hint of why that might be the case came when first seeing locusts devour vast tracts of vegetation on which numerous other creatures depend for their own livelihood. They devoured without replenishing and they did so even when human beings were desperately trying to stop them. The locusts ate for reasons that were natural. It is what locusts do. I did not know where that observation might lead. I did, however, begin to think that, whilst every human being has contributed to our global problem and is accountable, there is a much bigger picture that needed to be understood. It was one that went even deeper than would be otherwise assumed. I wanted, therefore, to find out what that 'bigger picture' was. All I knew was that it was somehow to do with that word 'natural'.

Testing ideas and insights

In order to spiral in a little further – and in order to open a hand more fully so that it can catch a ball – allow me now to explore the theme of accountability in a little more detail. I will do so by returning to the design processes in which I have been engaged on a multitude of occasions in my now long working life. For, I became convinced that they are directly relevant to the core questions that I am raising here. They were also pointers to the reason why life is as it is, locusts and all.

As I go into more detail, do ponder whether processes in your own life's work, as well as other arenas, may also be relevant. For, it just may be that they may help you provide other insights into our shared global predicament and how we should all respond. My reason for suggesting that is simply because we all live as part of life and it is life that needs help in order to live. Our own roles and contributions must, therefore, be toward unlocking the essence of a practical solution and not be further additions to the problem.

I have just used the phrase 'unlocking the essence of a practical solution'. Many designers agree that there is a sense in which the process of conceiving and then constructing a building is akin to a form of gestation. For, the core design idea is like a seed. It is sown in the privacy of a mind. That mind is then akin to a womb, where life can live. The seed of a design idea can only grow when it is recognised, explored, articulated and tested in discussion. Along the way, ever more focused rigour is necessary. That can happen by defining more clearly 'the essence', as well as the increasingly detailed implications, of the idea. That process can be one that often challenges the strength and consistency of the core design proposal. If it survives, something special can happen. The seed of an idea becomes a design 'solution', as a scheme that can be built and occupied.

As we have seen, that testing process includes accountability in the context of legal and regulatory processes and the laws and guidance notes they uphold. The outcome can then be the much-needed statutory and other approvals. If granted, construction can start, with a brief that led to a design idea now able to be built. When that happens, the gestation of a seed has led to a design that is equivalent to a child being born, having grown within the womb. I will now use a phrase that is crucial as we journey forward. As with a child, 'it is a gift unwrapped'. The resultant scheme is then one that can be built and almost come alive when used.

That 'birth' is then a transitional point from what has been essentially hidden to what will be fully seen, related to and inhabited as a place for people. Throughout that gestational journey that core idea was, in a sense, an intention. It was a theory that could be tested, not just conceptually, but when anticipating actual practice. That essentially context based 'artistic' process is then defined by an evidence based 'scientific' process, focused on what must work, otherwise people could get hurt. That transition can only occur when the experience gained by people, often over generations, in a wide variety of contexts has one focus. It is that the 'babe' is 'born' and 'born well'.

In my work arena, it is when the seed of an idea becomes a building that can be occupied. That occupied scheme is then:

a. The consequence of a process. As well as:

b. A new addition to an inevitably changed context. That outcome may then become:

c. A context for another new process that involves others. It can be one that, in turn, can lead to further change and other outcomes.

As I write, the forthcoming 2020 November Presidential election may or may not lead to such a change. Just as a neighbour may or may not conclude to add an extension to their house. Whatever the outcomes, all our lives will be affected.

Relate those examples to our individual lives. As soon as a child is conceived, the context changes for the mother, as well as for others who are close. That child, when born, then becomes the reason for a series of responses. Those responses can then lead to processes that can also lead to new contexts. I am a granddad of five months and the impact of Ella's birth has been huge. Both Jenny and I are seeing that occur almost every day. With each new context, there are then consequences following. New opportunities may arise, with new ideas about different ways of living. For many grandparents that has led to them living closer to their grandchildren. Will that happen for Jenny and me? I do not know.

Whether as an idea or as a person, a seed sown can, therefore, have consequences in new contexts. If that happens, there is then an opportunity for new consequences and seeds being sown.

As a specific example, these pages are, for me, the consequence of seeds of ideas that were sown several decades ago, with very tangible outcomes following. They are also a gathered insight into those consequences. When as a book, they are then a further seed that may lead to new ideas and other outcomes. Many are unknown to me. Such is the privilege that each of us has when being:

a. Part of life into which seeds can be sown;

b. With consequences that can change our Earth's flow of history and even when in:

c. A context that appears to be final in an end to viable life on this our planetary home.

I am mentioning this now, because of the encouragement that I have felt when noting the remarkable consistencies that are there in the whole of life. For, in all the severe negatives, something is going on now and has been for millennia. It is a something that permeates and even undergirds the whole of life. Those consistencies are there all around us, as well as within us. They are in my life, which in turn includes my workplace. Those consistencies then embrace and infuse your life, including any workplace and any arena you are in. Your leisure interests will, almost certainly, be different to mine. Nevertheless, I am sure those consistencies are still there.

At minimum, they are, once again, that:

a. I am me and you are you;

b. We are both alive;

c. We can both relate to others and we can both belong. Yet:

d. We are also like life itself in that a day will come when we will die.

But, as I write, that end has not yet come. As a result, there is precious time. This issue then is a question. It is:

. How should we use every moment, whilst there is time?

That question applies to every dimension of our lives, which includes our workplace. As a result, themes that I discovered are evident in my former role as an Architect and Planner can then be seen to be relevant to the much bigger context in which we all find ourselves. That context is the whole of life and its flow of history.

The implication then is that the same principle also applies to your own life and every arena you inhabit. It too is relevant to our understanding of the whole of life and a flow of history that is moving toward an end. That huge context is then another form of clothing on us all. It is clothing that is worn on a moment by moment basis.

As I felt the challenge when discovering that consistency, the sense of intrigue that I have mentioned kept growing. That sense of intrigue was work-life focused. It referenced Architecture and design. It was about the design relationship between people and places, but I knew that it was also about even more. As I have suggested, the journey that ensued eventually led to totally unexpected consequences when my spiralling-in process reached its conclusion. The effect was total, with me being overwhelmed, so much so that I was momentarily dazzled and unable to speak.

That new context then led to a spiralling-out journey that later enabled me to understand why life is as it is. As a result:

a. My work life provided a womb-like context within which the seed of a way of seeing life was sown;

b. That seed grew to eventually be born, albeit in a most unexpected way and with an outcome that continues to inspire and motivate me today;

c. The resultant way of seeing and understanding life has then helped me define ever more fully that motivation, when designing places for people;

d. It has also enabled me to not just discern, but also begin to live theories about why the whole of life is as it is.

You may well have already done the same in the context of your own workplace and other processes. If not, do step back and explore what may be possible. For, my expectation is that your conclusions will be well worth while sharing with others, which is my goal here.

Not in a vacuum

As you have seen, my own workplace could, at times, be traumatic. To have to close my architectural practice was not my intention. Its painful demise did, however, lead to a seed being sown for what could now be, with what was akin to a birth then following. For, a new era in my life was born. There was the need for immense care in nurturing that new era during the early months. That led to a move to live near Oxford and enrolling in the programme toward a Professional Doctorate, with the opportunity for more objective, as well as rigorous, testing of what were still young ideas that needed to grow. That growth eventually led to a re-engagement 'in the big wide world' of world views, understood and applied in practice.

As a result, my London Water City and New Eco Crystal Palace strategies became ever more relevant, as well as deliverable. Writing as I am here is, therefore, part of that 'new birth' and that enlarging process. Its context continues to be the prospect of a dying Earth. Once again, do keep assessing whether you think the predicament that I am suggesting is real. If your conclusion is that it is not, do then say. If you felt able, for my sake as well as yours, do also allow others to then test that conclusion. Whatever the outcome, do set out your own thoughts on what life on Earth is all about in the context of the future, the present and the past.

For, one thing is certain. It is that, by reading these pages, you exist, just as I also, at least, existed whilst I wrote them. You may not think the fact of the existence of a life leads to any form of question, with the ones I am raising being unnecessary. If so, it is because you are like me and privileged as someone with free-will to make decisions and choose. Nevertheless, even if only to merely help me, do set out your own view of life, so that there can be a response from others. For, as I know well, it will be a seed sown into a needy context that can lead to the most unexpected consequences. More even than that, we can all benefit from knowing of your thoughts on life's theory applied.

Your own seed ideas sown may grow with consequences that are beyond anyone's imagining, such is the privilege of being alive as a global community of people. For, we can all think, relate together, understand and explore and make contributions to life's ongoing flow of history. As a result, we are all able to play a role in enabling our planetary home to live fully and meaningfully for as long as is possible and do so whilst there is time.

There is then one other consistency that I noted as a form of amplification on themes already touched on. It is also evident in my work arena and, from there, I suspect in the whole of life. It is that the seed of an idea can only become an outcome – as in, for example, a design, a building or a strategy – if there is a context that:

a. Exists;

b. Is accessible in terms of understanding and;

c. Is then able to be varied.

I have mentioned that because I have found designing in a vacuum to be difficult. For, there is no point of reference or context. That realisation is then a form of affirmation from an experienced designer of the need not only for a brief as a reason why for every design decision. It is also for a specific context for that brief to be defined. That context has then to be people, a place of places and at a specific point in a flow of history comprising time.

That principle always remains. It does not only apply at the beginning of a design and construction process. It is ongoing and it is hands-on. I am a dad and I know how hands on nurturing a child is from the moment of birth. I am now being reminded of that fact of life, when watching my granddaughter grow. Hands on engagement that requires preparation is key to any form of nurturing, with planning ahead being constantly needed. Every stage of the process, therefore, demands a high degree of personal involvement. If there is not, the child's growth could be hindered or worse.

With that in mind, hiding away from immediate and real-life issues is definitely not an option. Thinking those issues do not involve each one of us or that they will, somehow, go away only increases the risk of far worse.

As a result, not only are an understanding of context and personal engagement key as a way forward concerning our global predicament, there is also one further foundational fact of design life that is as formative as it is key to that big picture. I have alluded to it before and the time is now right to 'hammer it home'. It is that buildings do not 'just happen'. A lot of work is involved in both the design and construction processes, with often very capable groups of highly skilled people. Each is, in turn, part of a network of specialists that can be extensive. None of their capabilities have just happened. All will have roots in seed-sown, nurtured and grown learning, as well as testing through application, often over decades and centuries if not millennia. To make a design come into being in our own era is only possible because of the work of others now and in eras before.

A question then arises. It is:

. If that is what is needed for a building to be constructed, what was the 'it did not just happen' context for the whole of life?

My own tentative response became somewhat heartfelt as the implications of the question dawned. It was that we in life are the beneficiaries of an enormous amount of preparation, thought, care and pre-planning that occurred before life was first 'seeded' and hence before life as we now know it was 'born'. More even than that awesome prospect, life has lived for millennia, which means that care has not ceased. It has remained, with the notional possibility that now neither is being appreciated nor honoured.

Next time you see a mum with a baby or a dad playing football with his son. Do imagine the care being shown. Just as next time you turn a tap on or switch on your computer, do imagine the detailed and complex flow of history that led to those, now, simple actions. Do then imagine the enormous scale of the preparation-to-seed idea-to-outcomes that enable so many other actions we all take each day. Then multiply each into billions of other contexts that comprise the whole of life.

Both you and I are, as a result, the beneficiaries of an incalculable legacy of pre-planning, delivery and nurtured care every day of our lives. For, every component and dimension of the life we live is a response that has already been made to a brief that had a context. Every moment can be experienced because of decisions made and actions taken, leading to multiple consequences following that have then been ongoing. The scale and detail of that rooted pre-planning and outworking in constructed delivery is then as vast as they are consistent and interdependent.

The phrase 'component of life' is a little impersonal. Nevertheless, I am very aware that I am a living component within the vast building or 'mechanism' that is life. I am equally aware that you are a precious living component of that same life generating wonder too. Indeed, we all are.

More even than that privilege, we are all then privileged to be able to live out the same pre-planning, seed of ideas sowing principle in everything we do.

. What on Earth is going on here?!

The exclamation mark is there with the question, not least, because the seeds we all sow lead to other 'components' as outcomes that will add to the whole of life. Each will then affect the overall functioning and well-being of this our life enabling planetary home. For, each cannot but play a role for good or with the opposite effect, especially in the context of the deadly predicament we all face.

Whether globally or as individuals, the terminal, life-will-end context is one that, it would seem, we all share. With that in mind, I will suggest a definition of 'good' that is very practical. It can be summarised in a sequence that I have already used. It is 'adding more time to our lives and to the life of our Earth'. As a result, 'bad' can be defined as contributing to an acceleration toward a personal as well as global end.

I have highlighted my own work arena. As you have seen, my view is also that no arena in life should be exempt from the themes I am exploring here. For, the same principles could apply in every dimension of life, far beyond any workplace. If my view of the predicament we face is real, it will have to occupy all our daily lives and on a minute by minute, as well as even second by second, basis.

As I have suggested, the Coronavirus pandemic is but a foretaste of what is to come, with 'no arena being exempt'. That total embrace should even include making a cake, playing football, washing up, as well as listening to – and even composing – a piece of music. As a result, in every arena I live, the following applies:

a. Understanding our context;

b. Preparing a response;

c. Conceiving a seed of an idea, then:

d. Testing and nurturing its growth, thereby leading to:

e. An eventual outcome as a positive contribution to life and not the opposite.

Our further context is the well-being of our planetary home. My suggestion then is that it is a well-being that can only be understood and met if its reason for being, its brief and hence life's reason why is known and lived. Once again, I will come back to this proposal in a lot more detail as we journey forward. For, now my goal is to enable a hand to open and be ready to catch a special ball in the form of an answer to the core question 'why?'

At this point, I am very aware that I have used words such as 'good' and 'bad', as well as 'success' and 'failure', with pointers toward definitions for each. My ultimate definition can only but be set in the context of that reason why. For, all those words have a context in life as we live it. Life is also in the context of death. As a result, each word requires a definition that is set in the context of the demise we are all facing personally and, it would seem, globally. A key question then rises, which is:

. Is the definition of 'good', 'bad', 'success' and 'failure' only about, say, adding more time or not to our lives and that of our planetary home or is there something more?

My response is to say that their ultimate definitions can only be seen in the context of, what became for me, a definite sensing of a 'something more'. That was even when I did not know what it was. I now know, with its identity being embraced by my answer to the positive, core questions I have asked, summarised as 'why?'.

When now knowing of that 'something more', I am then even more aware of my own 'failure' on a daily basis and, not least, when my architectural practice demised. More on that anon. In the meantime, you may find it helpful to note down your own definitions of that word, as well as those for the words 'good', 'bad' and 'success'. You may also find it helpful to set each in the context of events in your own life, just as I have in mine. It may then be that our two insights can be the welcomed contributions as we all:

a. Seek to make sense of why life is as it is and:

b. Respond positively as individuals to the prospect of a personal end and:

c. Be able to do the same, but together, in the context of an impending global demise.

For the goal must be that those definitions enable each one of us to address the predicament we all now face and do so with the maximum positivity. With that in mind, do feel able to add the following questions to the list that is now, of necessity, getting rather long. They are:

. What is the most accurate definition of success?

. What is failure?

. Why is there success and why is there failure in life?

. What is the reference point for knowing what is positive and what is negative?

There are then yet others as a form of Pandora's Box opens to reveal more inter-related questions. They include:

. Why does success tend to feel good and failure the opposite, namely, bad?

. What is 'good' and what is 'bad'?

As you have seen, I have found that the meaning of all those words always has a context that leads to a brief, with pre-planning concerning every aspect of life. That context has dimensions that can be personal, social, technical, environmental, and, from there, a list of other points of reference that is potentially limitless. All are relevant to who we are, where and when we live. That context also embraces our relationships, skills and capabilities, as well as the fact that we are all part of a flow of history, rooted in the past, alive in the present, with a consequential future coming toward us. Along the way, I am also very aware that every context can then lead to immense variables that, in turn, have limitless ramifications.

This is when knowing that a positive response to each might lead to added time or less for life here on Earth. For me, it is also when knowing that there is something far more. As a result, the magnitude of the task I am suggesting we all give ourselves becomes self-evident. It could be summarised in two words that I have already used. They are not final, but are:

a. 'Limitless' and:

b. 'Overwhelming'.

Just as any definition of any word can be constraining, so another consequence can be that such a definition is almost impossible unless we understand why life exists and is in the context of death. With that potential dilemma in mind, I have been tempted on many occasions to echo the view shared by the friend I mentioned previously. It was that it is impossible for anyone to answer the core question I have raised, which is:

LIFE, WHAT ON EARTH IS IT ALL ABOUT?

Nevertheless, the very fact that life exists akin to a building meant, for me, that there was, to use my architectural term, 'a brief'. There was a reason for the constructed design that is life. Assisted by a way of thinking implicit in my Architect's training, my view was that had to be the case. The seemingly inaccessible had, therefore, to be accessible. The seemingly impossible had also to be possible. That is why I kept on going. That journey then took on an urgency of colossal proportions as the deadly serious predicament, we all have now to face, increasingly registered.

As you will see, I then sought out and gained a core answer through a remarkable sequence of circumstances and interventions. As a result, each subsequent design project became an opportunity to live the answer to that core question. Once again, each scheme has then to be set in the context of the need to earn a living for my family and for the people working with me. I have failed in that latter arena. Do, therefore, look at the projects I am showing you in the context of:

a. Success and failure, especially my own;

b. My goal of enabling a sense of belonging, set in the context of:

c. The predicament we all face and:

d. As we journey toward my own answer to the ultimate question 'why?'

Do so when also noting that, despite my failure, each project, each scheme and each strategy had come into being as a result of that emerging understanding why our world is as it is. They are, therefore, in a sense, expressions of a world view that embraced failure. They are, therefore, specifics that are also set in the context of one totality.

There is then a sense in which we are all not just components, but personal participants, as well as even stakeholders, in all our lives. Together we are all then privileged to be participants in the whole of life, with a past, present and future. We are also able to play our role in fulfilling life's pre-prepared brief and reason why. We are then privileged to be able to do so whilst there is time. The effect of all our actions is ongoing right up to the moment when our personal and shared end arrives.

As you have seen, certain of my reasons for highlighting the parallels with my workplace are because:

a. Building projects and hence places in which people can live, work and enjoy their leisure time do not just happen.

They can only come into being if:

b. The designer is knowingly and positively working within contexts that already exist.

With those insights in mind, allow me now to take these themes another step further.

Heading Six

A DESIGN BRIEF AND CLOTHING

Image 21: More than just a porch

Some of the themes that I am highlighting may initially seem, not only obvious, but also possibly invisible and even irrelevant. Nevertheless, they do exist. They are also fundamental to the way we live our lives.

When I began discovering and assembling each, a multi-dimensional brief, for me, came within reach as criteria for a world view about life that worked. When also remembering my analogy of catching a cricket ball at the end of Heading Two, it was then as if my hand was opening, with fingers getting ready to catch a ball. It was a ball that is the reason why for life's existence in the form that it is. For that to happen, my hand had to echo the shape of the ball. As a result, even before the ball hit my hand, its content and size were being anticipated.

As you ponder the themes so far, do continue to have that analogy in mind. Allow me then to take that parallel one small step further. For, when I did catch the ball that is a world view that works, my expectation was that I would then be able to play my role in what some have called 'the game of life'.

When that happened, my further expectancy was that such a 'caught and held' world view would, in turn, help me define the essence of the design of any scheme when serving others and do so with ever greater relevancy. For, that way of seeing life should encapsulate the DNA and core information that makes all our lives, not just live, but also be special. My goal then was that its content could inform my own contributions to the big picture for us all. For, the core DNA should enable me to discern and 'brass rub' into being the seed of a design idea that was ever more consistent with life's brief and reason why. If and when that happened, I would then be able to pass that ball on to others.

Once received, that design seed could grow and be seen to be part of our ongoing 'game of life'. At this point, the parallel with a game of cricket has limitations. For, a player and a team must respond to a time limit in the game, but after its end there could be another opportunity to engage. In the real life context I have been exploring, there will not be an opportunity to do that. For, it would seem, the end will be the end.

Allow me now to return to my own work arena as part of life. The seed of a design idea is a response to a brief and the brief always has a context. That idea cannot initially be seen, but it is known to the designer. There can often be a feeling of excitement when that seed is sown. He or she may then describe it in words or in a sketch, as the unseen becomes visible when shown to the client. It is then assessed, with responses given, as the clothes of a design are 'tried on' by the one who will 'wear' it. Changes are often made, as the spiralling-in process embraces the many decisions that have to be made before construction of the design can commence.

That inward journey can, at times, be tortuous but is necessary before a spiral-out process can commence. That outward journey starts when tenders to building contractors are sought and construction starts. It continues when a client occupies and inhabits the completed building. When at college, that process can appear to be simple, but in practice it is can also be the opposite. That is because of the ever-enlarging number of criteria that need to be added to the core brief given by the client. As context to brief changes, so does design to construction. Indeed, that sequence can occur on many occasions.

I have mentioned some of the inputs set by Planning and Building Regulations. They are but two of many. Do then relate that spiral-in and spiral-out design and habitation sequence to how the whole of life came into being. It then becomes clear that we are all occupying a 'building' that is the outcome of an equivalent process from briefing to habitation of immense complexity, as well as one that has been remarkably consistent.

From my experience when working as an Architect, assembling the criteria for a scheme was, at times, challenging. Along the way, it could also be overwhelming and disorientating. For some designers, that leads to an inability to make decisions. For others, an exclusion of some criteria can follow in order to establish, what was felt to be, a manageable and defined context.

As the brief is assembled, potential design solutions are often explored, but always with a light touch. For, what is important is to get a design that fits the needs of the client being served. Often a client had to vary his or her understanding of those needs during early conversations in the briefing process. As a result, the more accurate the criteria, the greater likelihood of an outcome that works in day to day practice. The spiralling-in process toward a design answer is, as a result, once again akin to a hand being opened ready to catch the ball.

It is only when the biggest possible picture has been grasped that a 'ball' in the form of a building that is capable of viability can be designed and built. The words 'viable' and 'viability' would then have, as their point of reference, the fullest possible insight into the design's context, purpose and, hence, its reason why in life.

If that multi-layered, at times seemingly overwhelming, picture is the case in my work arena, my suggestion is that it is also relevant to every corner of the biggest 'building', which is the whole of life. As a result, it has also applied to every component of the design that is the life we all live here on our Earth. That principle, in turn, must include everything that is in our vast host cosmos.

It is then as if, not just one building, but a city comprising billions of highly complex equivalents has come into being. It is as if every near and far place is a designed and constructed entity, rooted in a brief that was then framed by a context. If that is the case, the context that led to that brief must be of ultimate proportions. For, not only is everything in life inter-connected and mutually dependent, so is life's relationship with how it all came into being.

The process from context to brief, brief to design, design to construction and construction to occupation – by us and so many other living beings – is also all interconnected and mutually dependent.

Logically, it also happened as a sequence. As a result:

a. Just as a many-layered context is needed to assess the schemes that I am showing you, so an ultimate and far more complex context is needed, if we are to understand why life is as it is and, from there, what on Earth life is all about;

b. Just as each scheme is a result of a way of seeing our world, so each is a window into that 'ultimate ... far more'. It is a something 'far more' that had:

c. Understood a context to then define the brief – and hence the reason why – for the 'design and construction' of the whole of life, in all of its immense detail, its inter-related complexity, as well as its remarkable consistencies;

d. That process has then been so successful that living beings exist and have been able to occupy the outcome. As a result:

e. The context and brief that existed before life did lead to a design seed being sown and consequential design and construction processes, that:

f. In turn led to a vast, cosmic building that embraced an Earth that could be inhabited.

With that backcloth in mind, my goal became finding out what that colossal and almost infinitely detailed brief was for the whole of life. More even than that. It was, also to find out what was the context that led to the brief that, in turn, led to life. Logically, both the context and the brief existed before life existed. Both, therefore, were already there before our cosmos and our Earth came into being.

. But how could that context and brief be known?

I initially had no answer. My goal, however, became to know what that context was and how that brief came into being. For, it was only then that I could understand why the constructed design of 'life' is as it is. It was only then that I could understand life's reason why in a way that might, in turn, inform my approach to designing places for people.

Clearly, that goal was built on the assumption that there was a context and there was a brief. It was, however, an assumption that I concluded had to be a fact, if 'life' is to make any sort of practical sense, whilst there is time.

As you have seen, so much of my thinking and my life's work have their roots in my student days. That formative era also has roots in the lives of the family of my birth. Their roots were then in an ever-larger context, with each being intertwined. I am sure you will be able to say the same in your context. For me, an exploration of my own ever bigger picture, having started in my youth, has continued throughout each of the several decades since. Indeed, any understanding of my life and all our lives as one total picture is an ongoing process. For, there is so much that is already there, waiting to learn.

Even as I write, I am learning and adding to my understanding. On each Step along this journey, I have been able to add more and more substance to what was initially a seed-like, as well as embryonic, framework of theory outworked in practice. Again, it was one that was formed during those early student days. That ongoing process has happened as I have tested its principles by applying them in real life, client serving practice.

When picturing that process from a seed to maturity, there then is another dimension I should now add to those already outlined. For, I have indeed discovered that there is always something more. As one door opened, with a room full of ideas able to be explored, another door was then ahead waiting to open. I have never found that experience frustrating. I have only found it to be the opposite. For, my response was always one that I have already mentioned. It was of ever greater intrigue. It was also one that became – and I will use that other word again – tantalising.

. Why was opening doors to new insights tantalising?

It was because, wherever I looked, there was so much evidence of there being something so far, far more that, whatever it was must be nothing less than amazing. It was not only a context and a brief. Nor was it even the answer to the question why. It was the sense of certainty that there was a thinking source for all that exists and, from there, an originator of that reason why and all that then followed. The resultant brief and the seed of the idea that is life was then nurtured to become the whole of life as we now know it. As a result, there was a context for every detail in the whole of life. That context was a 'client' that had decided to commission a huge scheme.

When that thought first came, I hardly knew what I was thinking. What I did know was that there was something already there waiting to be known. Indeed, it even felt as if that something wanted to be known. It was as if the design language of life I was exploring was saying just that: 'I am here to be known'.

More even than that, it was as if, in the growing number of consistent themes that I was exploring in the constructed design that is life, that 'to be known' included answers to the questions I was raising. They were already there in what I was seeing, hearing, learning, touching and feeling, so was their source. I did not know what they were. What I did know was they were already there in the midst and beyond everything that our senses can perceive. It was not long before I concluded that that source was the reason why for life and was, as a result, life's originator.

I then began to realise that the key to understanding the many inter-related answers was as simple as it was profound. I have briefly mentioned it. It was to see that originating source as a form of client. It was then to ask questions of that client and do so positively, expecting answers. They would be answers that would enable me to discern the seed of a solution to the need to know life's reason why. It was one that could then grow into a cosmic design that had been built and viably occupied. It was also a cosmic design that could then host our Earth, as well as very much smaller buildings designed by former Architects like me.

As a result, the life I am still privileged to live is part of a living building that had an originator that, in turn, had a context for its design and construction brief. Whatever that originator was, it knew the answers to the questions now being raised. They were already there waiting to be received and understood. My expectation was also that the originator would know why all of life appears to be in the process of dying. The implications of that notional prospect were, therefore, vast.

Allow me now to take that possibility a little further. For, it soon became apparent, not only that those answers existed, but also that their first expression came when the first 'foundations' equivalent of life were 'dug'. Others followed and all in eras long before my own. They had already happened in our Earth and cosmos's distant past. That realisation, in turn, magnified the sense of tantalised intrigue I was feeling. For, I had a growing sense that I was exploring realms that not only already existed, they did so with the direct involvement of the originator. I was, as a result, on a journey of discovery concerning the very source of life.

I even gave that client source a name. It was 'the life essence'. The building that is life belonged to whatever that 'life essence' was and it did so with an intimacy that I found to be very moving. As a result:

a. That 'life essence' was now at the centre of my two spiral diagrams and:

b. From there, my journey became one of seeking to know what that 'life essence' was. It was also to do so with the goal of:

c. Understanding and then living the reason for life.

It was also becoming a journey, not just of identifying, but one of seeing that 'life essence'. It was even with the expectation of meeting whatever it was and then receiving from it the answer to the question 'why'.

There was then a further consequence that I am hesitant to describe, as it may be misunderstood – but here goes.

It was of a growing feeling of being humbled, with a certain humility then following. For, I was beginning to realise that many people had almost certainly already seen what I was seeking. Some had even used the word 'truth', with their insights then being deemed to be 'true'. Once again, both are words that need to be defined. I will be bold and attempt to do so in due course, but not just yet. At this point on our journey, I will simply say that it is a way of seeing and understanding life that works in both theory and in practice. It is also a world view that makes sense of everything that has been and is, as well as can be and will be. It is, therefore, fundamentally a highly practical framework for living and for life, even when knowing that life is in the context of death.

When I look back, after wondering whether I was the first to ask the many questions I have listed here, I soon realised that many, many people, long before me and long before our own era have been asking the same questions. Indeed, they have asked many more and have done so in far greater depth than I have done. What I found very moving was that a large number had discerned the consistencies I was only just beginning to be aware of and note. They had done so, not just decades or hundreds of years ago, their insights into theory applied went back millennia. I will say more in due course, but the answers they discerned helped shape the lives of thousands of other people, as well as many places. So much so that whole communities changed, as did nations and even continents around our world.

I learned of examples during my student days, thanks to illustrated talks given with enthusiasm by lecturers at my college, the Architectural Association. They had often followed visits around the UK and abroad, with a lecture theatre then being a window to the world. I will introduce you to some of those lecturers as we journey forward and say a little more then. As far as I know, none were thinking in terms of spiral-in and spiral-out diagrams, nor of any life essence. Yet, all were fascinated by life and, in their own special way, were as intrigued and even as excited as I was. As a result, other words and phrases may have been in their minds. I do not know.

For now, it became evident that there was a consequence of seeing consistent themes in the daily lives of the communities involved. Even when centuries and millennia before our own, there was a sense in which an understanding of their present had been set in the context of assumed certainties, including about their past. They had done so with a commitment to the future that was nothing less than astonishing. That commitment was evident, even when knowing that, as individuals, they were unlikely to see that future come into being. For, a sense of a known past seemed to infuse their present with a confidence that enabled them to anticipate the future ahead. Remarkably, it was not with fear or dread, but with positive expectation. It was also with death being faced and even embraced. The impression then generated was that their lives had been enormously enriched as a result, as had the communities of which they were a part.

Their lives, therefore, were about, what one might call, a theoretical world view which met the criteria that are emerging here. It was one that had a consistent and meaningful, as well as expressed, context that was past and future, beyond their own lifetime. Significantly, that way of seeing and of living embraced the logical probability of an originator of the seed of life. That originator was then involved in a subsequent flow of history, focused on their present and then their future.

One consequence was that they applied the insights they had gained and sought to make each live. They then did so often on a scale and with a degree of confidence that left me with a sense of awe. It was an awe not just of buildings and how they are constructed. It was also of a world view that was able to lead to and generate those outcomes. It was a way of seeing that embraced the source of life, as well as the whole of life. Once again, more on this anon. For, there is a bigger and ever deeper context that we are moving toward. At this stage in our own journey, I will offer some encouragement and say that, in principle at least, it is one that has already been understood. There will be dimensions previously known that I do not know and may never know, just as there may be new insights in the pages here.

For, there is then one certainty in life. It is that every human being that has ever lived and will live has and will be on a journey. It is a journey that has a personal beginning and will have a personal end. The prospect of such a beginning and an end also seems to apply to our Earth. In our own era, we are realising that. One insight from my student observation of other world views in our distant past was that a global beginning and an end were both assumed.

Allow me now, therefore, to offer a summary thought. It is that many from eras long before my own had already come to the conclusion that there was something akin to a 'hands on' originator that had brought every dimension of life into being, with that originator even anticipating an end. I was, therefore, merely seeking to catch up.

I have used the word, 'clothing', in the heading here, just as I have on several occasions in the text. I will now say a little more and do so, once again, through the eyes of someone well acquainted with designing buildings and, hence, places for people.

The design outcomes of the world view that is the 'ball' we are getting ready to catch were my own responses to an ever-enlarging number of questions. Each was rooted in my emerging understanding a positive 'why?' for the whole of life. As a result of my questions, I was also beginning to realise the relevance of that short question, not only in my life, but also in the lives, probably, of millions of others before my own. The consequence was that the now ever-present sense of intrigue grew and grew.

I not only wanted, but also started to long for an understanding of the answer to the ultimate question 'why?' I specifically wanted to know the originating source of that reason 'why?' and, from there, the identity of the life essence. It was to know the ultimate context for everything. It was an 'everything' in life that was:

a. Enormously complex and seemingly limitless and:

b. At times tearful and at others joyful because it was:

c. A belonging-referenced life in which living and dying were intertwined. It is also:

d. An existence in which we are all small, but:

e. At least to each other, very precious parts.

Allow me now to take one step further the architectural design principles that I have touched on. They are of context, briefing, idea seed sowing, nurturing to a completed building as well as occupation. It is to point to the originator's relationship to the life we live in this awesome cosmos. Initially, it is also then to say that:

EVERY PLACE WE EVER EXPERIENCE IS AKIN TO CLOTHING ON THE LIVES OF PEOPLE

For, that is what clothing on our bodies can do. It provides an interface context that enables each one of us to engage in life. Clothing does so by enabling us to perform activities that can, in turn, enable new futures to unfold for the wearer.

Clothing is, as a result:

a. Personal and should fit its occupants;

b. It should be comfortable in the context of its specific purpose;

c. It must help us do what we seek to do;

d. When that happens, in a sense, we live life with greater effect;

e. We can do so enabled by our clothes;

f. We can then engage and move forward in our lives;

g. Clothing can also be seen and say something of the person within, as well as that person's purposes. It can also:

h. Enable each one of us to do things individually and together that we may have otherwise found difficult, if not impossible, to do.

The kit worn by a football player is one of many examples, as is a warm overcoat or a spacesuit worn by an astronaut.

Clothes can also be specific to a context that is sometimes not conducive to living, such as rain, cold weather and extreme heat. They can then have an attenuating purpose, such as keeping the wearer dry, as well as warm in the winter and cool in the summer.

When seen as buildings, clothes can enable us to share in activities with others, say in a sports hall. Instead of being negative when the world outside is wet, windy or cold, hot or dry, by being within the clothing, the relationship can be positive. Those built clothes can then help us relate to other people in a place and for purposes we share. Such clothes can also enable each one of us to be in a relationship that is as positive as possible in, what can often be, a multi-dimensional context.

Even a small project can be clothes. Allow me now, therefore, to say a little more about one of the ladies who owned the porch in the photograph in Image 21. Her name was Mary Lister. With another lady of a similar age called Elsie Baker, she lived in a house that was somewhat chilly. I met them both soon after my college years finished, with my newly formed office being very much in its early stages. Both were retired and quite elderly. As a result, they especially felt draughts through their front door. As clothing, that part of their home was inadequate for their needs. A glass and timber porch, with an outside door, was then inserted, thereby enabling both ladies to keep warm and enjoy even more their much-loved home.

The porch, as a project, therefore, had a context that had both positive and negative dimensions. The positive was a greatly loved home. The negative was a cold draught that undermined their well-being. The brief given was to enable a negative to become a positive, but with one proviso. Any changes must not lessen the character of the main house, but somehow to enhance it. Mary and Elsie had seen examples where that was not the case and they were worried.

As a design, what was inserted was a tangible answer to a specific problem being experienced by the occupants. The new porch then helped their home be more energy efficient. By being made mainly of glass, it also was, in effect, a small conservatory. Part of the enjoyment of the home was the garden, which could now come almost into the house. The project was small. It, therefore, made a tiny contribution to a global response to the huge predicament we all face concerning the well-being of our Earth. It was, nevertheless, a response that sought to honour the sense belonging felt by two special ladies, both of whom were in the latter years of their lives. Every moment spent there counted.

As previously highlighted, such belonging could have been seen to be in contradiction to a dying Earth. The outcome in a porch was, however, a positive response to both dimensions of that seeming disparity.

As a result, I see this small project as being ‘more than just a porch’. It is an insight into how we can all journey forward, as THE BIGGEST CHALLENGE before us all becomes ever more real. It also became a project that had as its core point of reference my answer to the big question why, which is our ultimate challenge. I will say more about that in due course. When doing so, I will let you know of Mary Lister’s response to a simple everyday scheme. For, that response proved, in its own way, to be a form of seed sown, with so much more that then grew to become reality. A key point now is simply to note:

a. The principle of places being akin to clothing within which people can belong and that:

b. If that belonging is not practical, as in a draughty house, it can be detrimental to human health, just as it can be to the health of our planetary home. And:

c. As a result, belonging and enabling our planet to remain healthy for as long as is possible need not be opposite. They can be a precious two that are mutually supportive as-one.

As I pondered that principle of clothing, another way of seeing started to come into focus. It not only embraced the contradiction I have highlighted. It also held ever bigger and deeper implications in response to the core questions I was asking. That new focus was an extension of a theme that I have recently mentioned. It initially took the form of another, perhaps, cumbersome question that, I felt, needed an answer. That question was:

. If every design of a place is seen as clothing on people, is life itself also clothing on whatever might be that originating something more?

I did not initially know the answer, but I found it a necessary question to ask. It was a question that did, however, become increasingly more intriguing, as its answer might be fundamental to so much more. Once again, when the answer came, it took me totally by surprise.

As with the example of a porch, my workplace goal was by now to address what were often specific inadequacies in places. That was when seeing places as clothing in which my clients lived, worked or enjoyed their leisure time. My response was to use emerging design skills to resolve those difficulties and, thereby, enable a new future for people living within their built clothing. You have been introduced to one of many projects in a porch. Several more examples of relatively small schemes will follow as we journey Step by Step.

The same principle later applied to larger projects and, finally, to the major development strategies that I have begun to highlight. All were responses to practical problems. Each was, therefore, a proposal that sought to address real-life, complex, as well often difficult, situations with many negatives to change toward being positives. As that happened, my desire was that not only belonging between people and a place ensued, but also seconds of time were added to the life of our planetary home.

Each can also be seen in the public arena. Hence visual images are of real people in real places. The situations described can, therefore, be seen. As a result, the solutions being tabled can demonstrate, or otherwise, whether my own emerging theoretical framework about life is viable in practice. Do, therefore, assess whether each is akin to clothing that is personal and social, as well as environmentally beneficial. I will also add economically and even politically helpful as part of one total approach – on and on. That 'on and on' can then include arenas that you will know far better than I, because you are you and not me. Once again, do table your own contexts.

When looking at outcomes, do also test the credibility of the world view that begins to rise through these pages. It may even be sensed from the journey so far. For, that rising way of seeing led to each proposal. Please do so from your perspective and, hence, with the insights that you will have. Once again, the context for both of us is the planetary predicament we all face, as one that affects me, just as it affects you and every 'you and me'.

The way I responded to that predicament has already had consequences; the same principle applies to the way you have responded in your own context. I am responsible and accountable for my own subsequent interventions, just as you are for yours. That accountability has an ever-larger context, of which everyone else on Earth is a part. For, as I have shared, none of us is exempt. As a result, we are all in this together in success as well as failure.

Indeed, everything we do affects everyone else, including those who are dear to me and to you. There is then a sense in which our shared accountability is also part of our ultimate shared context. It is the existence of life and, from there, its reason why. Layer upon layer, everything in life is then like clothing on us all, as well as whatever life's originating why is all about.

So far, alongside a porch in Images 19 and 21, I have highlighted two large projects in the form of a series of green energy generating inhabited bridges in the East Thames region in Image 14 and a New Eco Crystal Palace in South London, as in Image 20. My reason for doing so is, in part, because each context told initially of inadequate, even wrong, relationships between people in a place. Solutions were then needed to turn negatives into positives as contributions to an ongoing flow of life here on Earth.

For the first in a London Water City the negative issues were:

a. The big social and economic divide caused by the River Thames;

b. Much-needed homes and other accommodation for a fast-growing population;

c. The need to protect existing and new communities living in a large and vulnerable urban region from flooding due to climate change and:

d. To get ready to live in a world where the need for green energy generation from renewable sources must be the 'norm', if we are not to accelerate the non-viability of our planetary home.

My response was a form of water-based, inhabited clothing, with principles that could be exported around the UK and many comparable contexts around the world.

For the second in a New Eco Crystal Palace, a land-based community of people had felt and still feels the loss of its former, world renowned namesake, the 1854 Crystal Palace. That community is well able to be world stage. It can do so in a way that showcases, very positively, what our global future has to look like. Whilst being rooted in a belonging that is deep in our shared past, every community around our world might then be able to benefit. That is especially when knowing that a global network of ethnicities emanates from South London that is far reaching, with a flow of ideas, thought processes and practical information that can lead to a beneficial effect that is world-wide.

That New Eco Crystal Palace could be a media-based phenomenon to which a large proportion of our global community could belong. It could then embody a future that addresses as positively as is possible the profoundly negative predicament our world is now facing.

The third scheme was tiny in comparison in a porch. It was clothing on a two-person community of elderly people, who were living in a much loved, but nevertheless, cold and draughty house that was the home where they belonged. The issue there was how to remedy that negative in a way that did not undermine the precious sense of belonging that they felt when living there.

The predicament that we all face is, therefore, directly relevant to both the large communities on London's east and south sides and one that comprised two elderly people. There was then a sense in which even large communities comprised many that were small. As a result, the issues being addressed affected every elderly person, everyone who is middle aged and everyone who is also younger still. For, they also affect every child and even every seed in every womb that is growing toward birth. Those issues may even lead to a series of negatives that would prevent precious seeds being sown, thereby removing any possibility of a future.

It would seem the predicament we all face is there because of decisions that have already been taken over millennia, as well as ones taken in more recent eras. It is getting worse by the day because of other decisions being taken now.

As a result of those past and present contexts our future is dire. As a result:

a. Every person and every place on planet Earth are inextricably involved;

b. Generations before us are responsible and accountable and so are we in our era;

c. We all need to recognise that fact of life, if we are all to help each other make sense of what is happening now.

For that to happen – and I am looking in a mirror here – there needs to be a degree of shared humility that has, perhaps, been lacking throughout human history. It is only then that we can listen to each other and:

a. Determine a world view that works in practice and from there:

b. Know how we should relate together with:

c. The goal of being able to respond as positively as possible to the deadly predicament we face, with:

d. An abundance of practical solutions, such as an insulating porch and a green energy generating inhabited bridge being part of that response.

With that sequence in mind, your own critiques of my thinking and the work I have done can be part of that overall goal of positivity. Just as any critiques of your thinking and work can lead to the same.

My awareness of my own accountability makes me ask that you be as rigorous in your critique of my approach as you would be of your own. For, the reality is that we all do need each other, both in terms of thinking that leads to solutions and in ensuring that those solutions are delivered as effectively as possible.

As I have shared, my own thinking is rooted in insights that I summarised in a series of diagrams, several of which I will show under the next Heading Seven. Later, you will also see more of the schemes that are my response to the contradiction and the predicament we all face. When looking at the diagrams and the other images, do note a dimension that intrigued me greatly. It is the relevance of geometries and especially triangles and circles. For, each enabled me to access seed-like solutions to ever larger and more complex problems.

As a result, each geometry was a tool that enabled me to seek out positive outcomes in negative contexts. You will also see something else that I found even more intriguing. For, I began to be aware that those geometries seemed to be everywhere in life. As you critique the approach that I am in the process of outlining, do test that particular insight, as its accuracy or not is key to what I will table as our journey continues to its conclusion, Step by Step.

Alongside triangles and circles, you will find spirals returning. For, each helped me understand the processes involved in designing people- and place-based building projects, set in the context of belonging and a dying Earth. I found them helpful when seeking to understand, not only the structure within life itself, but also why we face such an agonised contradiction. It was a dynamic that, in turn, led to me being given an insight into life's reason why, as well as even the identity of life's originator. It was also a dynamic that helped me to enter the pain caused by the enormous tragedy, of which we are all a part.

Throughout, one context has remained constant. It is that people and places exist, as do occupied buildings, that are akin to clothes. If the 'clothes' do not fit, a negative effect can result. Frustration can follow for those within, with a form of ripple effect that can, for example, change the atmosphere of a street or town. Equally, if the people do not fit the clothes, they will inevitably tear, with failure following. It would seem that the biggest 'tear' in history has now become visible, with that 'tear' leading to non-viability here on Earth.

With that in mind, you may find the following questions helpful to ponder:

. What if the clothing that is life does not fit the wearer?

. What if the wearer does not realise that the clothing does not fit?

. What if the wearer then realises that his or her attitude to the clothes needs to change?

From there, when seeing belonging as place-based clothing fitting the lives of people:

. Is a lack of people and place belonging leading to the demise of both the people and the place that is life here on our Earth?

As with so many questions, I did not initially have answers, but I do now. That is why these pages now exist, for my goal is to share what I know with you. You can then try on my world view clothes and, from there, see whether they fit.

Allow me now to make that process a little more practical and, once again, do so in my own work arena.

When I left college and began my work in architectural practice, one insight became clear. It was that theory alone about design was inadequate. Action was also needed, for the issues being faced by clients were highly physical, often with radical changes needed, say, to the layout of a house. The cost involved could be significant, both financially and in disruption. This was especially when remedying difficult people-and-place situations in the life, say, of a family living within clothes that did not fit. Advocate the wrong solution and the problem could get worse. That is why it was always important to first step back and try to understand what was wrong, as well as what was right. The client may know, but sometimes he or she was only aware that something was wrong, without knowing why.

My first response was always, therefore, to ask questions so that two outcomes could occur. They were:

a. That what is wrong is understood, defined and recognised, as well as what was right, so that:

b. A design solution could be sought that turned negatives into positives.

The next step in that problem-solving process was often a diagram of activities that the to-be-changed building was to enable. The intended occupier, say a family, then tried on the ideas implicit in the diagrams. If they were pointing in a direction that might fit, a sketch proposal based on the diagrams followed. If those initial design clothes did not fit, it was back to the drawing board or computer. If they only partially fitted, changes would then be made. That may happen on several occasions as the design is varied so that, like clothing, the final scheme did fit the wearer.

Architects often call that process 'design development'. For, if the essence of an idea in a sketch proposal works, more discussion and testing then enables its seed-like form to grow. As I trust will be appreciated, it is important that the process is not rushed, so that there can be as much certainty as possible that the thinking, thoroughly tested, is found to be right. As a relevant aside, that formative stage can be exciting in what can be a long and, at times, arduous, 'birth'. For, it is crucial that the scheme is as close to being right as is possible. Smiles always came when the clothing appeared to fit.

For, if a design does not fit the life of the client when it is built, difficulties will become apparent. They will do so in day to day use. Instead of problems being resolved and with new opportunities generated, the opposite would then have happened. A difficult situation has been made worse. Interestingly, I have also found that changes in the design of the house must not only fit the people, the way the occupants use it must also be right. For, clothing on people is a two-way relationship.

If that two-way thinking outworked in action is right, one outcome can be a family enjoying living in a house that was once a source of frustration. Their home might then be greatly loved, valued and enjoyed: happy people living in a happy place. Not only can a house and a home acquire as a 'smile', but so can a street and even a town, with benefit rippling beyond. That same principle can, I am sure, even apply to our planetary home, our Earth.

If the core thinking is wrong, the opposite to benefit can be the case, with a lost opportunity being the outcome and an already difficult situation made even worse. That is why I am saying we must 'get it right' for our Earth, because, if we do not, the end will come ever more quickly and painfully.

If we get the thinking right, a very practical belonging for people in a global place can come into being. That can only happen if an understanding about how negatives can lead to positives is tested, with reassurance following. The seed of a viable idea can then mature, with good outcomes following.

Do hold that practical analogy in mind as you test my thinking and as you test yours. For, we are all occupiers of an Earth that is akin to a house that has design and construction problems. As a result, it is collapsing and even dying, as are its inhabitants, which is tragic. What adds to the magnitude of that tragedy is that the relationship between the clothes and the wearer is two way. For, it would seem the problem exists, at least in substantial part, because of the approach of the wearer to the clothes worn. As a result, it is important to ask the following questions, when seeing the condition of our Earth's built clothing as a response to a view of what life is all about. They are:

. Does that world view clothing fit life's many wearers in practice?

. If that clothing is leading to negatives, is the time right to consider changing that world view?

If the answer is 'yes':

. Are alterations only needed, or should a far more radical solution be considered?

. If so, perhaps the time is right to consider a different approach that could mean starting again?

As a result, because the problem we are facing is so huge, now is the time to recognise that many current world views are not working. It is then to assess what is wrong and move toward a world view that works in practice. If that happens, a way forward could be discerned and implemented that can lead to both:

a. A deeper belonging for people and the place that is our planetary home and:

b. More time to enjoy and live that precious two way belonging.

My suggestion, therefore, is that a beneficial people- and place-based belonging becomes our shared goal for our Earth at this critical stage in our history.

As you know, I am now in my 70s. Many of the projects referred to here we completed decades ago. Each client and wearer are, as a result, in a good position to know whether the design continued to be clothes that fitted, beyond the initial period of use. That is why I concluded to revisit a number and meet many of the people we had served. In some situations, my original clients had moved, with others now in occupation. In several, I was able to gain the response not just of one, but also of several generations. When doing so, my point of reference was:

. Had the scheme enabled a people- and place-based sense of belonging; if it had, was it still doing so?

Insights gained, both negative and positive, then became lessons learned as part of my own ongoing journey. I am pleased to say that almost all responses were positive. Having said that, there was one exception. For, one situation had changed from being a positive solution to a difficult inherited problem, when the scheme was first completed, to becoming four decades later very painfully the opposite. I will say more as we journey forward. When doing so, I will highlight both ends of the spectrum of:

a. How inherited failure became success for one generation, only to then find:

b. That success changed to become failure for the generation that followed.

I will also share my response to that change, as part of our journey forward.

In the meantime, one key outcome of contacting past clients was the renewal of the friendships. As a result of a form of living research, relationships were deepened, with new relationships forged with people I had not met before. A consequence was belonging enabled through my place of work in the past being enlarged in the present. When that happened, I was reminded of the growth over many years in the shared belonging that my parents engendered when their customers visited their corner shop. Through my workplace, belonging has also first been built, then renewed and even enlarged when I visited each project.

That positive outcome was not certain. It could have been the opposite. Every visit, therefore, held a risk. When a memory from the past was enlivened in the present, there was then the prospect of both indwelling the future. Once again, do hold onto that sequence as we journey forward. For, what is in prospect for all of us is, at best, a limited future, even when extended. It is then to suggest that, even when knowing that context, memories enlivened in the present of belongings previously known are precious and to be treasured – and for reasons that I will explain as we journey forward.

As you have seen, the subject I am exploring here specifically brings in references to the design relationship between people and places. Each is set in the context of my own growing understanding of that relationship, with specific projects I have been involved in being the outcome. As a result, all those insights and projects have one common denominator. It is a bloke called Ray Hall (!). The context for each is then, inevitably, my own parentally seeded and personal history-framed identity, leading to my own maturing as a person and in my workplace. The same principle applies to who I have become in the years since.

That ongoing flow of history has then affected other people and impacted my work as a designer of places. The people that have influenced me and the experiences that have shaped my life can, therefore, be seen to live within each of those schemes. There is then a sense in which each scheme has become a part of not only who I am, but also the people with whom I belong. My suggestion is that the same sequence applies to you, your different background and, from there, the affect you have had on other people and places, as well as vice versa.

With that in mind, I trust you can see why I concluded to show photographs of me in my early years, even when some are amusing with me needing a haircut, as in Image 6. For, I know that the head under those ungroomed locks was, at the time, wrestling with many of the issues I am exploring here. Each of the photographs you will see also has a specific context, which is inseparable from who I was and who I am now. If you were writing your own equivalent of these pages, your photographs would also carry a context that is personal to you. You would then be charting your own life's journey, just as I am here.

My daughters are obviously much younger than me. When they reach my lengthening years, they may decide to set out their thoughts about their own life's journey. Those thoughts may include what each thinks life is all about. If the predicament I have highlighted is accurate, their context some 35 years from now will be more acute than now. Indeed, that may prove to be an understatement. As a result, the pressure on them to discern viable answers to their own questions could be severe.

Their questions may include mine. They may not. I do not know. What I do know is that they will, almost certainly, have at their disposal far more information than I have been able to harness. Instead of my relatively small collection of images, they may instead have many thousands to choose from. What they write may even be able to include videos that are interactive, or even stage sets to enter, thanks to whatever communication/information systems that have, by that time, been invented. It may be possible to do that now, without me knowing.

Whatever format, each would bring back many memories that capture a life lived and the many moments of joy, as well as tears, that they would have known. One moment will link to another, as a total picture then starts to emerge, as pieces of a history jigsaw puzzle. That bigger picture will, no doubt, be accessible by a potentially limitless number of 'friends' or otherwise. An ever broadening and deepening, insight into their lives as part of life itself may then rise. If everybody was able to do that, the collective impact on our world could be significant, life changing as well as potentially overwhelming.

I am mentioning this now because the decisions we are making are already affecting their future. Our way of seeing the world is inevitably, even now, affecting their experience of life. In the future it will also be information that they can retrieve. Our expressed world view is, therefore, already informing theirs. Crucially, it was also to be remembered. As a result:

a. Even though the response we have to our global predicament in our current era may not necessarily determine theirs, it will frame everything they think and do;

b. If we are fundamentally wrong, their thinking processes and decisions could be hampered, with one outcome being a lessened ability to slow down an accelerating global decline. However:

c. If our thoughts and actions are, at their core, fundamentally right, then the opposite can happen. More time could be added to life here on Earth. It would be time that would otherwise be lost and:

d. That would be a greatly appreciated remembrance.

Having shared that, my expectation is that so much of the information needed to help us know what is wrong and what is right is already available in our own era. If it is not already known, it is waiting to be understood, with the ability to do so growing exponentially. As a result:

a. More positive actions are possible, just as are the opposite and:

b. 'Success', in terms of adding time to the life of our planet, or 'failure' when not doing so will steadily become more explicit day by day, with accumulations of each year by year. There may also, on many occasions, be:

c. Utter confusion by some as to what those words, 'success' and 'failure', mean, but the reference point will be clear. It is simple survival personally as well as globally.

A further outcome will be ever more heightened pressure, as the implications of the task become more fully evident, as well as critical, with the prospect of panic following. A sense of fear could fill the air, making the global response to the current Coronavirus pandemic but a foretaste. Lessons learned during the pandemic could lead to more information being available that could then exacerbate the situation. A form of global chaos could be the outcome. That is why it is so important that we all define what we mean by 'success' and 'failure' and do so as a priority, with mechanisms set in place to enable positivity and not the opposite.

As a way of getting ready, that is what I am seeking to do through these pages. It is to contribute toward a definition of 'success' and of 'failure'. When knowing of the need for such a definition, I will in due course table a strategic, governance and participation way of enabling that here in the UK and around our world.

With that in mind, I will now say that, for me, success and failure are already out there in the buildings that I and my teams have designed, so much so that I cannot 'un-design' them. Having been built, they can be demolished. Whilst they stand, each exists and does so separate from me. To use the term inherent in a Professional Doctorate programme, all are what is defined as being a 'public work'. Each is, therefore, affecting the lives of not just a small number of people, but potentially many, directly and indirectly, with an ongoing ripple effect. Just as none of those projects exists in isolation, so nothing you have thought and done is 'an island' with no consequential effect. I will say it again, the same principle then applies to everybody.

For, everything we all think and do is part of our shared life and is hence accessible by someone somewhere, as well as affecting everyone everywhere. That is the case now and, I am sure, will be even more so for the generations that will succeed our own. Whether I am alive or not, that will be the case and potentially exponentially so. Three questions then resurface with an ever-deeper relevance:

. Why are none of our lives 'islands'?

. Why are we privileged to share deep relationships in life?

. Why is it that everything we do affects others in some way and potentially even more so as life's flow of history journeys on, even beyond our own limited lifetimes?

Those questions and so many others will become ever more relevant as the end approaches. For, there is a sense in which the stricken clothing that is the whole of life is in the process of, not just pressuring, but also imprisoning each of us. So much so that even now, we are all, in a sense, being crushed by its weight.

I trust you will appreciate that I am not saying this lightly. It is, however, necessary, not only because it is real, but also if my own suggested way forward is to be understood, grasped and then lived. The diagrams that I have referred to now follow, as we spiral-in and as a hand opens in readiness for catching a ball that is the world view that I will table.

Heading Seven

DIAGRAMS

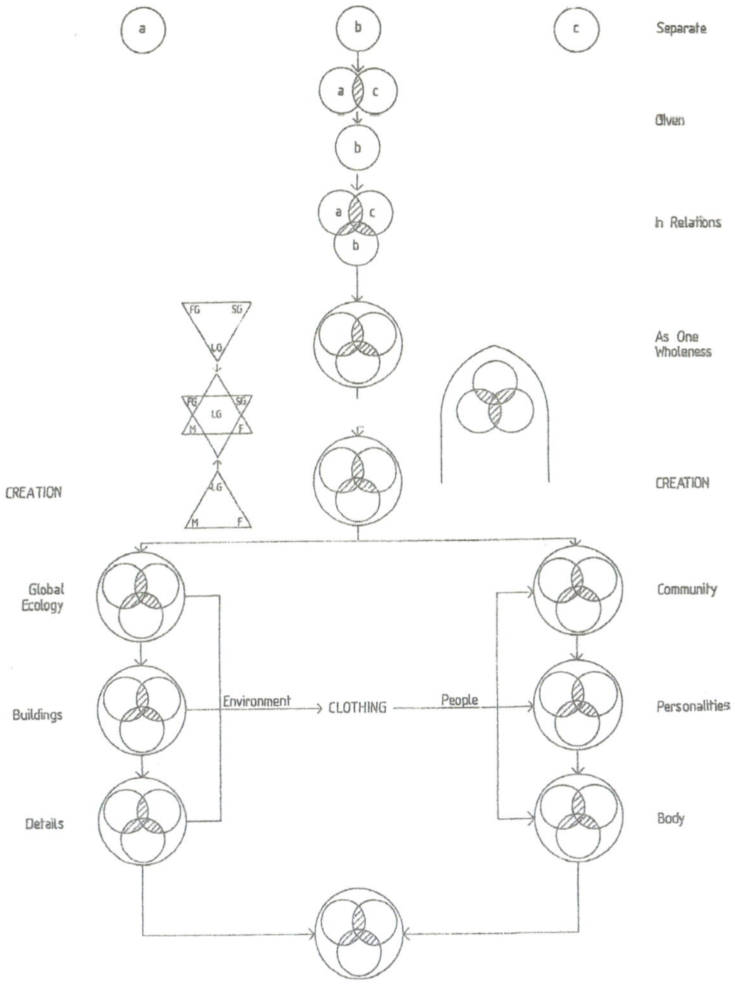

Image 22

Each diagram became an expression of an emerging theory about life

I was then amazed how practical they were in my work arenas

As insights into life that is past, present and future

In life, we all experience 'ups' and 'downs', as well as, by whatever definition, 'success' and 'failure'. Each influences the way we make decisions. That decision making then becomes inseparable from who we are individually and together as a global community. That is why my own life and my own experiences are inseparable from the explorations through these pages, as I seek to harness lessons learned.

One still relatively recent 'down' for me, rooted in 'failure', was the collapse in 2007 of the small multidisciplinary practice I had founded some 34 years previously. As I have shared, that failure was especially painful, because the practice's name, 'People and Places', embodied what I saw as my life's goal. The same applied to its logo. For, it told of what was, in a sense, my life's vision. As you know, my health then failed due to the strain when trying to avoid closure. My over-riding recollection of the aftermath, however, is not one of anxiety, but of peace. This was partly because I was unable to move and do anything. There was also a sense of relief, for my very hectic and responsible work life was over.

Allow me to give you a little more insight into what happened. I will do so as an illustration of how an early student diagram, in Image 23, became a living reality.

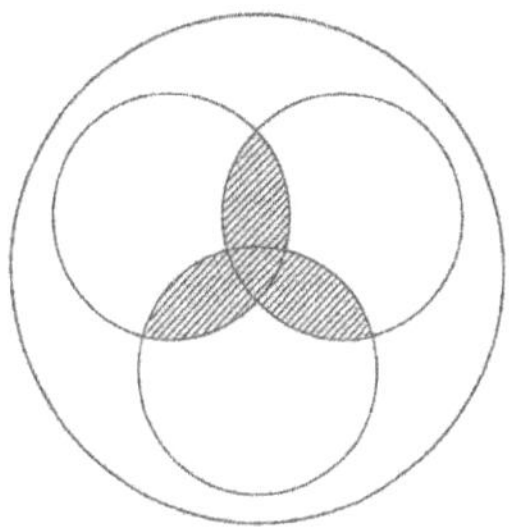

Image 23: Three circles overlapping as one

When my practice closed and my health almost demised, belonging relationships with others quickly became very hands-on. Jenny not only collected me from my office, she became my support. Once my difficulty was correctly diagnosed, with my daughters, Becs and Claire, she then helped nurture my slow recovery.

At the same time, my accountant, Peter Willans, stepped in to deal with many of the technical and procedural issues involved in the voluntary liquidation of the company. A former work colleague, Jeremy Lodge, helped my few remaining clients. At the same time, a close friend, John Ling, who I met many years previously as a client, became a solid source of selfless support. His home was near Bournemouth, but he was often there by my side in London. If you have experienced such care, you will understand when I say that tears bubble inside as I type their names.

A definite 'down' and 'failure' had led to a very tangible and practical expression of support. All were rooted in relationships that were now focused on the goal of positive outcomes rising out of a situation that was fundamentally negative. It was a belonging that enabled me to slowly recover and enter a new era, now able to dawn. It was also a belonging of people in a relationship as one, with a shared and selfless focus, which, I am grateful to say, was me. The diagram in Image 23 tells of that precious dynamic.

With that example of practical belonging in mind, allow me now to set out the series of diagrams I assembled when as a student, with each leading to that core summary diagram. I will also use them on other occasions as we journey forward. The first is in Image 24:

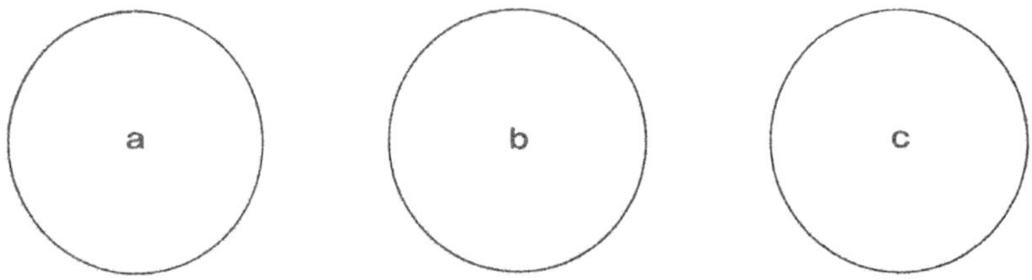

Image 24: A sequence of three circles, with each telling of a person or a part

In my early thinking, circle 'a' represented, for example, my mum as a unique person. Circle 'c' told of my dad as another different, as well as unique, human being. The second circle 'b' was first my sister and then me. Neither my sister nor I was my mum. Nor were we my dad. We were both individuals quite separate from my parents.

Mum and dad, in turn, were two identifiably separate individuals, who shared in a relationship as a two-as-one. They formalised that relationship in marriage. The next diagram in Image 25 tells of that relationship. It was one of a shared belonging, with one person being in a bonded relationship with another, with the overlap of the circles telling of that bond:

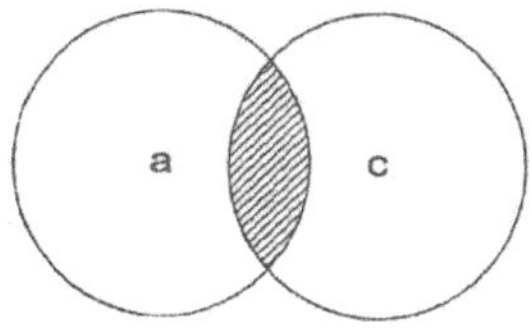

Image 25: Two circles as two people or parts in a relationship

As a two-as-one, they then gave their relationship to another, when they embraced my sister even before she was born, as in Image 26:

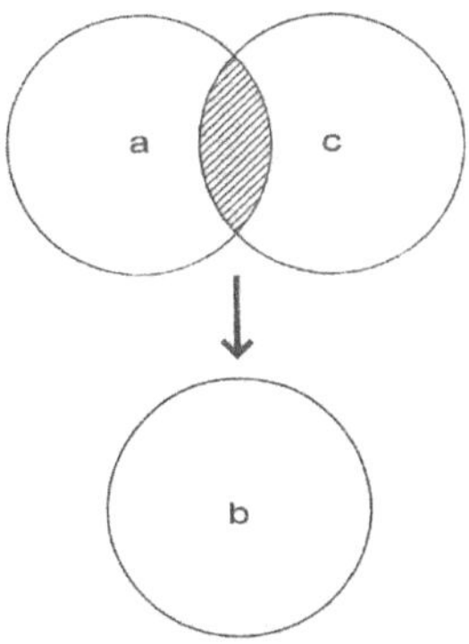

Image 26: Two circles in relationship seeking to relate to a third

Together, they then became something special. For, they became a three-as-one relationship, with each, in a sense, indwelling the other and bonded together for life. The next diagram tells of that union. It, therefore, tells of an enlarged, even selfless, belonging.

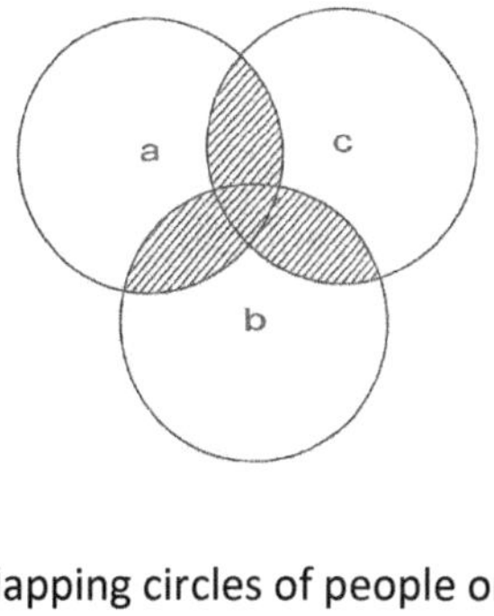

Image 27: Three overlapping circles of people or parts in relationship

Something equally special then followed. For, their shared relationship was now not just of three circles overlapping, a new entity had also come into being and it too had its own identity. That new identity had a generic name. It was and is 'a family'. The diagram in Image 28, with three overlapping circles inside one, tells of that relationship, with the outer circle telling of that new identity. I then became another part of that family. As a result, I grew discovering its presence on a daily basis. I then benefited from its practicality, when aged 59, in 2007. It was when seeing the response from my own family and friends to my office closing and my health failing:

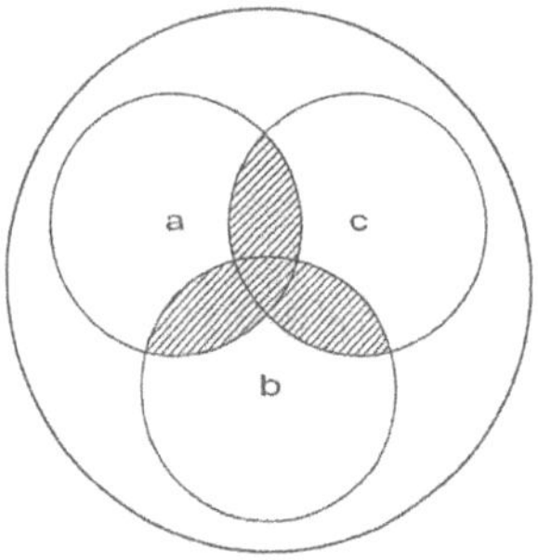

Image 28: Three circles overlapping in a relationship as one

As I have shared, soon after my mum and dad decided to adopt my sister, they were then able to conceive me. When, I later learned of this, I began to see two-as-one embracing a third as being:

a. Intrinsically tangible, even solid;

b. In part self-focused, in that mum and dad desired a child, as well as:

c. Selfless, because two-as-one had deliberately changed to consciously become a three-as-one.

I will keep coming back to those principles as we progress forward. For, they are crucially important in the big picture I am exploring here.

In my parents' family context, one consequence was that I became another 'b' in the diagram in Image 23 and Image 28, alongside my greatly welcomed and loved sister. We four then became an enlarged family, with a unique identity that can, once again, be represented by the outer circle in the diagram. That outer circle of belonging was, in turn, able to relate to others, with an ever-larger sequence of relationships and belongings becoming part of our shared lives.

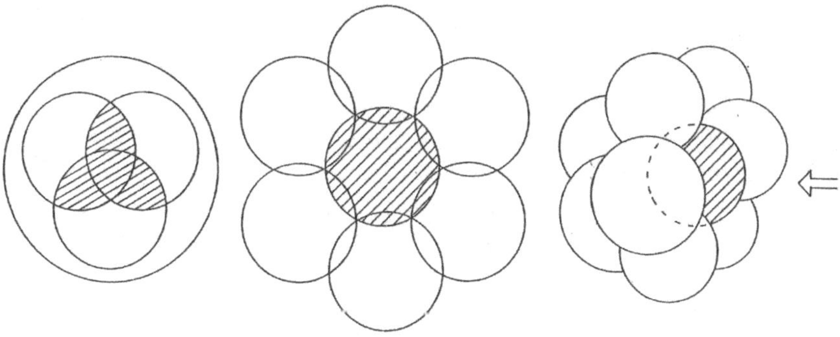

Image 29: A sequence of key subsequent diagrams telling of parts in relationship as one

The three separate circles overlapping to become a three-as-one is then in Image 29 and Diagram A. The individual people and the relationship we all shared as a new identity all had a name. It was 'Jessie', 'Norman', 'Barbara' and 'Ray'. They were names that told of personal identities, but they were not in a sequence nor in a line. A radical change had occurred. For, each separate circle had not only mutually overlapped in a relationship, together, they had become as one within a new outer circle. That new bigger identity then also had a name. It was the 'Hall' family, as represented by the outer circle that embraced the individual circles of identities and relationships within.

The relationships shared within that new identity are then represented by hatched lines in the overlaps of each of those inner circles. In Diagram B, the hatched circle represents the Hall family, with more circles added that represent other people known to us. Do note the overlaps of adjacent circles around the central circle. As an example, they told of the relationships shared by customers focused on my mum and dad's family-based shop. They later told of relationships in my office and with people, such as Peter Willans and John Ling. As a result, what was emerging was an understanding of the dynamic and the design of a wide variety of communities. Crucially, each came into being when there was a shared focus such as a shop, a family and an office, or someone like me in need.

Diagram C in the sequence then takes that two-dimensional (2-D) format by making it three dimensional (3-D). That change from 2-D to 3-D prepared the way, as you will see, for very practical applications in practice and hence in the design of specific buildings. Do then note the arrow, which suggests a point of entry into the community the diagram represents. In the context of Merry Oak Stores, that entry point was the shop door, with my parents as hosts within.

By becoming as one with my parents, each customer then became as one with each member of our family.

It was thanks to those diagrams and the insights they represented that I was able to understand, first the design structure of my own family and a shop, as well as then an enlarging number of other contexts. They included even an early insight into the ecological structure of life here on Earth, as in Image 30.

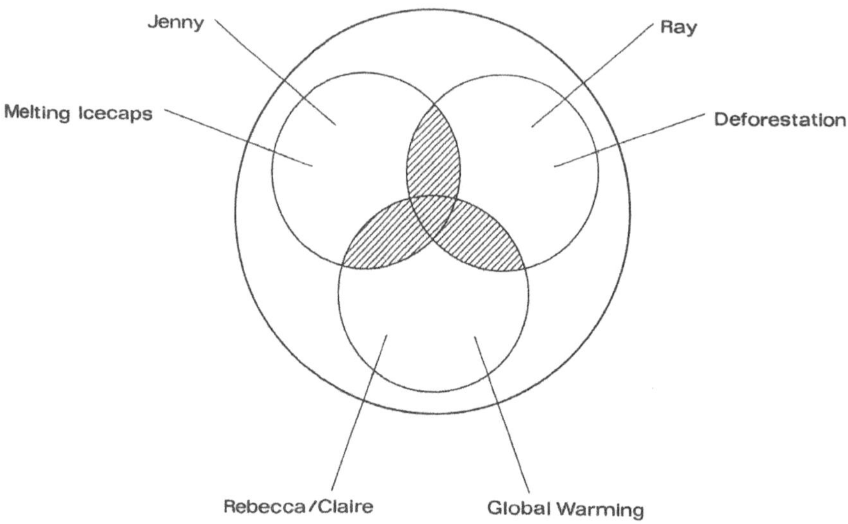

Image 30: Understanding the social and ecological dimensions of life

As a result, I became increasingly aware of the ever-bigger picture that I am pointing to through these pages. For, just as that same set of principles applied to a family and a group of friends, each with separate personalities and often with a shared interest, so they also applied to a football team, the mechanics of a car and an enjoyment of popular music, which in my era included The Beatles. I even began to see a vase of flowers with new eyes and the composition of colours and shapes in an oil painting.

Relationships and bonding one with another to become as one, therefore, was evident in many contexts. In human relationships, it happens when one person shares something of him or herself with another. It can happen with work colleagues, each with different identities and complementary skills. When they work together in a mutually supportive way, separate people relate and can become a unit. This occurs, especially, when they focus their capabilities on the service they can provide for their customers. Sports men and women can experience the same when they function as a team. For, football players, it is literally when they have the same 'goal' in mind!

Clearly the number of circles overlapping can be more than three, with Diagram B in Image 29 telling of that bonding of individuals around a shared identity and purpose.

As you have seen, I experienced how very practical those diagrams can be in a deeply personal way when I was ill in 2007. For, Diagram A came alive when Jenny, Becs and Claire made their shared focus helping me recover. Diagram B came alive when my good friends, Jeremy and Peter and John, gathered around, with their shared goal of helping me as a friend and colleague in difficulty. They protected and supported the Ray that they had come to know from their different perspectives and in their different contexts. As a result, I became for a period the hatched overlap of three circles and then the hatched circle embraced by six. Together, my family and work colleagues all then shared one focus, which was to help an ailing me.

I am sure you will appreciate that I find it very moving when remembering the bonded care and practical help each gave during, what was for me, a critical period of loss, adjustment and recovery in my life. I suspect you may have experienced something similar, possibly on several occasions, in your own life. If so, do hold onto those memories. For, lessons we can all learn from those experiences can help us to then prepare to address a shared focus, which is an Earth that is in debilitating need. That is because what is now upon us is as specific in its own way as the situation that I found myself facing those years ago in 2007, but on a vastly increased and ever-present scale.

As you have seen, the relationships that I have highlighted led to very practical outcomes. They were also focused. Each told of a belonging that, in a sense, came alive as a result. Each then led to a living belonging that then enabled me to continue to live from the age of 59 years to my now 72 years.

. How many more years will I live?

I do not know. I am, however, grateful for every week and month of every year that I am alive, whilst there is time. Nevertheless, I am certain that my own end will still come.

Allow me now to say a little more about my recovery process. For, in addition to my family and friends, doctors and nurses also applied their remarkable skills to enable me to survive and slowly regain my strength. They were able to do so, thanks to generation upon generation of people who had sought out solutions to health problems, often at great cost to themselves. The outcome here in the

UK is our awesome National Health Service. The diagrams I have shown you, therefore, embrace every one of those many relationships.

I will now add two more examples, not least because they will become relevant later in another context. For, those diagrams also point to relationships with near neighbours who were also close friends. They included Andy and Jill Parnham, who helped me empty my closed office of files and equipment. They did so box by box and it was a huge task. Due to my own lack of strength, all I could do was watch and give advice on what needed to be kept and what did not. If I remember rightly, we filled two skips of castaways. They and others then assembled each remaining box, ceiling high, in a large archive shed at the bottom of my garden. The goal was that, once I had recovered, there might be time when I could go through each and extract documents that may be relevant to any new future that may by then be unfolding.

As my strength slowly returned, I would look out of my bedroom window into our garden, with that shed in the distance. When doing so, I looked forward to re-entering the past world now hosted there. When I eventually did start to edit its contents, I could only manage an hour before tiredness overwhelmed. As the weeks went past, more time was added, as the ceiling became visible and the editing process moved forward. It has then taken 13 years for me to edit down to a remnant that I still need, with a lot of scanning of key documents along the way. That focusing process has, in turn, led to these pages.

As with other memories, do hold that editing and assembling process in mind as we journey, Step by Step, toward a climax. For, the conclusions I reached that I am exploring with you would not have been possible without that process having happened.

When returning to my diagrams, I had benefited from the overlap of my workplace, professional, family and friendship-based, as well as NHS, circles. During that crucial period, their focus was my vulnerable life. If they had not helped, I would not have been able to write one page, never mind all of these pages. Nor would I have been able to include the many images that you will see. For their love, care, protection and support enabled me, literally, to live during the years since. It is thanks to them that I also have whatever time now remains.

Once again, do then see that experience as a window to what is needed as we face a time limit to life here on Earth. For, when noting Diagrams A and B in Image 29, my suggestion is that the same principle applies for all of us here as we face an endangered future. Just as I would have died a premature death, so the same applies to the life of a planet that is our shared home. It too could die, when it could have lived for many more valuable years, with each ever more precious if they are lived in response to life's reason why.

In that context, do, therefore, ponder further my diagrams and the insights they hold. Do so, not only as a way of seeing your own context of friends and family, but also as a way of seeing our broader community. It is where groups of individual people and organisations can mutually support each other and do so with a focal point that is directly relevant to us all. It is of an Earth in serious trouble, with death just over the horizon, with limited time remaining.

As you ponder those diagrams, you may then see the relevance of your own networks in the context of the predicament that we all face. You may also see them 'come alive', as I did, whether in your neighbourhood, your town or in other regional, national and even international contexts. You may even begin to see each diagram, not only in sports teams, but also in orchestras and the functioning of our remarkable NHS, as well as global organisations such as the World Health Organization and the United Nations.

You may then see each as having a specific purpose and capability in enabling life to live and to do so for as long as is possible, whilst there is time.

If you have not already done so, you may also see what needs to happen in order to add that precious additional time. That could include the specific role you can play, as we all face the prospect of a dying Earth. For, the conclusion that I have reached is that, if we do not think and act as multiple circles overlapping as one, our Earth's end will come at the equivalent of my '2007', instead of at some point beyond my current '2020'. If we did think, live and act as a focused series of circles overlapping, there could not only be:

a. A much longer future ahead. It could also:

b. Be a much more meaningful future than if we had not become as one. It could, in turn, be:

c. One whereby all learn from past experiences and share lessons as gifts for others. If so, it is then to:

d. Have the opportunity to live the answers to the many questions starting with 'why'.

If that happens, a seed sown concerning belonging would have grown toward full maturity. It would have been our shared response to what is coming. Two more questions then arise. They are:

. What is the ultimate point of circles, in whatever form, overlapping as one?

And from there:

. What also is the point of caring for and helping others, if my life and all of life is going to die?

These are crucial questions that I am moving toward answering, with my hand opening as I get ready to catch and then throw that ball. At the heart of that answer is one core fact. It is that we human beings can bring healing in our own lives, just as we can bring healing in the lives of others. The same principle then applies to our Earth. We can add more valuable time, with an ability to participate positively. However, what we cannot ultimately do is prevent the inevitability of death. For, we cannot fully save our individual lives from death nor, I would suggest, can we save life itself.

We are, therefore, facing not just death, but the reason for death. That reason must be faced and it must be understood, if we are to make sense of both why there is life and why life is as it is.

My view is that the same core principle not only applies to my life and the life of our Earth, it may also apply even to our host cosmos. More on this anon.

Allow me now to say a little more about the implications of the 3-D Diagram C in Image 29. For, it tells of the 2-D circles in Diagram A and Diagram B, in a sense, 'coming alive' by changing into three dimensions. As a result:

a. The previously central circle becomes a sphere, with a series of surrounding spheres touching it, with:

b. That central sphere then giving shape to the many other adjacent, as well as enveloping, spheres. So much so that:

c. The resultant cluster is then able to relate to the outside world. It can do so by:

d. That outside world entering in via the arrow in that diagram. As a result:

e. The life of the central sphere is then accessible and able to be part of a much bigger context.

When relating that 3-D format to my illness, it was thanks to all the people around me that I was able to welcome the world back into my life. I was then able to look out, engage and receive, as well as live, a new future that came into being. Diagram C, therefore, tells of the restorative, new era dawning, power of shared belonging.

As that new era slowly began to dawn, for quite a while I had to simply lie on my bed. When I was able to stand, it was then that I looked out of my bedroom window to see that archive shed at the bottom of the garden. What I saw was something akin to a gift that had been wrapped by its wooden walls and felted roof. Within it was a working life of theory applied in practice that was waiting to be understood. To then realise that I may soon have the time to unwrap those many gifts was precious indeed. For, what was in prospect was not just a process of editing, as I made a large archive steadily smaller, it was also an opportunity to remember and extract lessons from the records within.

It was then even more than that. For, without the pressure of running a design practice, I now had the time when I could unwrap the gifts hidden within the many boxes and files. I could then assemble each insight gained as a gift that might be of help when given to others. It could be the gift of one life given to other lives. It would be a story telling of a journey of a lifetime. The diagram that told of two as one giving to a third in Image 26 then took on a new meaning. For, Ray and the contents of an archive shed could lead to a gift being given to others.

What was also special was that I now knew how precious and vulnerable my life had always been. It was then that I realised afresh that the same principle applies to all of our lives, even when we are not aware of it. For, I now knew that to be true in a practical way. For, I felt death coming toward me. As a result, I had not only gained an insight into the precarious position held by the whole of life, I had also felt something of the death that is approaching us all, just as it is our planetary home.

You may have already grasped that fact and felt that approach, but many may not have done so. For any who have not, do be assured that the day will come when you will feel it.

Having seen death approach, I am now more aware than ever that my life came into being and that it did do without my involvement. It was a gift. In 2007, 59 years after my birth, I then came close to losing it. By myself, I was not able to stop that end coming. Thanks to the help of so many, it was delayed. I did not expect what happened, but it did. Instead, when I look back, there was even the sense in which I had assumed – or should I say presumed – that I would live on and on. I knew that death would be there, but it was almost as if it was so far distant as not to be relevant. Tomorrow would, therefore, be another day. Just as next year will be another year. It was a very sobering experience to suddenly know that that may not be the case. In 2020, I am now certain that an end is coming and, just as it may be in years, so it could also be in weeks and even days, if not today.

In my own context, I was, in one moment, talking about work with my PA in the reception of our office. In the next, I was slumped on a chair, almost unable to move, saying to Kam, 'Please get Jenny'. Tears can rise when I remember those moments, so alive in my present is the knowledge of the fragility that I experienced in those years now past. Having been someone on whom many relied, I suddenly became very dependent on many others. I then slowly realised, ever more deeply, that I had always been dependent upon others, just as we all have been since our moment of conception and then birth.

More even than that, we are all 100% dependent upon the life of our Earth in order to live. As you know, I first realised that fact of life, when as a student. In my latter years, I now know it to be solidly true. For, what could have been a theory in my younger years has become real-life in day by day practice.

In 2007, I had also to face another fact. It was that the people with whom I shared a close relationship were having to face the possibility of me not recovering. Their belonging with me would, therefore, lead to their loss. At the time, my daughter, Claire, was in Costa Rica on, what was akin to, a student adventure programme when my health failed. She was often out of reach and did not know what had happened. She only learned of it when Jenny collected her from Gatwick Airport on her return. Tears poured forth as Jenny drove her home.

There is now the prospect of such a realisation hitting everyone known to us, as we all face the prospect that the whole of life has only a limited amount of time yet to live. Life will not continue forever. Our Earth will not even continue to be alive for millennia. It may not even be for centuries. For, there may, according to some, be only decades remaining. For, life's fragility and its many failures increasingly point to an end that could be only a small number of years away.

My expectation is, therefore, that there will come a moment when we will all, as a global community, collapse back in a chair. We may even want to say the equivalent of 'Please get Jenny'. If so, there will then be a dilemma. It can be summarised in a question. It is:

. Who can we say those words to if all the equivalents of Kam and Jenny have also collapsed into the same chair?

I am very grateful that my family and friends did not have to feel the pain of actual loss in 2007, nor in the months and the years that then followed. Nevertheless, that day will still come. For, life is constantly in the context of death.

I am equally grateful that, thanks to that experience, something was affirmed that I had known for many years. It was one of the early lessons learned I have shared here. It was that:

EVERYONE IS DIFFERENT, EVERYONE IS SPECIAL

AND WE ALL NEED EACH OTHER

Yet, even with that affirmation, the much bigger picture that I am exploring requires something more. For, I knew that even a fully bonded and mutually supportive local and global community will still find itself falling back into a chair, when we all face the death of our Earth. That question then returns. It is:

. Who will we all then ask to help?

The diagrams I have shown you so far tell of a shared need to belong. They are also akin to my cricketing hand opening, getting ready to catch a ball. With that in mind, do now have another look at my logo in Image 18. For, that shared need is there in graphical form, with one unique person relating to another and two-as-one then relating to a third. There is then a sense in which the shape of both a hand fully opened and that of the ball are also evident there. When first realising these principles several decades ago, I saw a very faint, but also defined, presence of a something far more, but that was all. For, again, I could not see its identity. I did, however, know it was there.

As I am sure you will appreciate, when remembering my student era, what had become a recognition of the importance of belonging, was then affirmed even more so by my illness decades later. It was that we have all, in some way, known the reality of circles overlapping as one in relationships with others. Yet, what is in prospect is that every belonging we have felt will stop and cease to live.

As I have shared, I felt a sense of peace when death seemed to approach. My response was, in part, as selfish as it was unexpected. For, whilst feeling that peace, I also knew that other people were deeply worried. Tears had fallen from eyes kept away from my view, in order not to worry me. I know other tears will fall, when this now ageing husband to my wife and dad to my daughters, as well as friend to others, reaches his end. If the situation was reversed and any member of my family was in danger, I would feel the same depth of worry and grief. I am sure you would feel the same in the context of your own belongings.

My suggestion then is that those tears will be dwarfed by the torrent that will pour forth uncontrollably when the pain of global loss registers.

For, I am very aware that, just as I need those close to me, so it is that they need me as well. I would be denying something special if I said otherwise. I am sure the same applies for you as well. I am then 100% certain that it will apply on a global scale when we all realise that 'one day there will not be another spring' for life here on Earth.

As I trust can be seen, I am exploring ever more deeply the themes of belonging and death for a series of specific reasons. One is as a context for many answers to so many questions why. Another is to anticipate a further context when my core reason why will need to be known, perhaps, as never before. It is to do so by giving insight into what is coming and to get ready. For, it is going to be nothing less than heart-breaking and painful beyond any comparison.

If anyone thinks otherwise, they are not facing reality.

More consistencies in life

In the photograph in Image 8, you gained a glimpse of my sister, Barbara, alongside me when were children. She died several years ago in her early sixties. I will never forget my uncontrollable yell of anguish when her daughter, Kate, rang to tell me of her departure. She was born on February 5th. Every year since she died, I continued to remember her birthday. For, not only was her life special, it was also a life that enabled me to be conceived and then to live for more years than she was able to know.

As I have emphasised, all our lives had a beginning. Having had to face my own mortality in 2007, I am now very aware that my life is finite, with an end not far away. I do not remember its beginning, but I can with certainty anticipate its completion. Its span occupies a small era in the life of, for example, the long-established market town of Witney, where I now live. That span is even smaller in the life of our nation. That is then dwarfed by the history of a global community that stretches around our world, with eras that go back for millennia. All our life spans are also tiny in the context of the life of our Earth.

Yet there is one consistency in each of these comparisons. It is the finiteness of life within time that has a beginning and an end.

Our planetary home, as a place, is also small, almost beyond tiny, in the context of a cosmos that really does seem to be limitless in size. The assumption by some is then that our Earth's life span is as tiny as its size in comparison.

Nevertheless, I exist within its minuteness. My life is also personal to me. It is a life that occupies a specific place in that vastness and as part of a flow of history that is also vast. It is a life that is known by others, who are personal and exist, even when as small as me. You too are personal and exist. You are also as small as I am in that much bigger picture, just as you are an individual distinct from me. You too can relate to many others, such as me. With that in mind, do now have a look at the photograph in Image 31. When it was taken, I was still a student, with hair long but now combed. I was holding my sister's first child in my arms and I was amazed.

You may have done the same and felt that same sense of utter amazement that this new little life exists at all.

Image 31: My sister's son is called Cristian

Inevitably, Cristian is not now a babe. For, he is in his 40s and has grown somewhat and could probably hold me in his arms! He is also now married to Elizabeth and is a businessman in South Africa customising 4x4s. They are well into their own life's journey, just as we all are. As with yours and mine, his life's journey also had a beginning and has continued until now, with many more years, I trust, still to come. We are very close, despite the long distance to Cape Town where he lives.

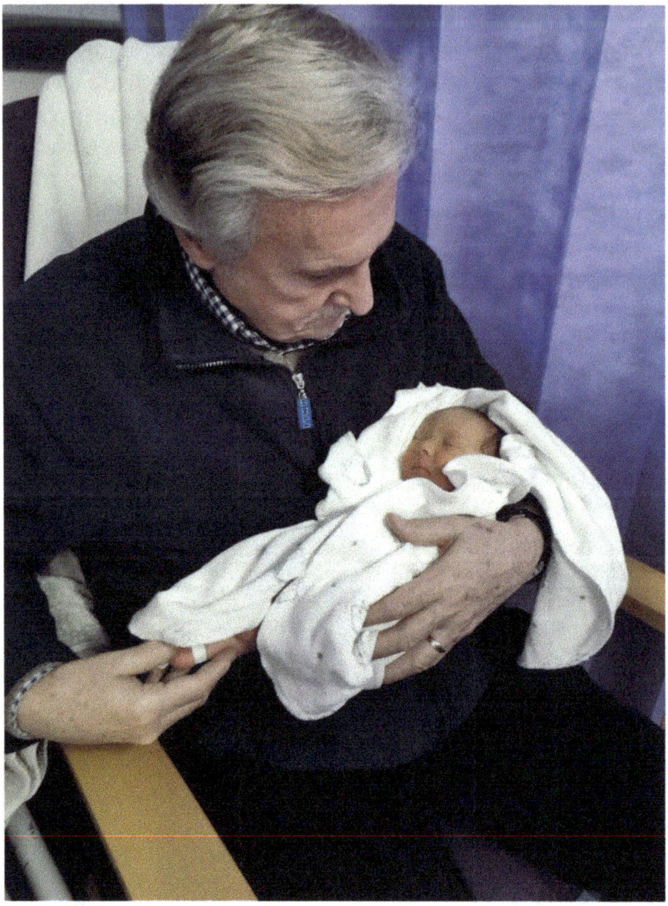

Image 32: 40-plus years later, Ella Sophia is now in my arms

In Image 32, there is a photograph of me only a matter of months ago. I am holding my daughter's newly born child, whose name is Ella Sophia. I was, once again, feeling that same sense of utter amazement I felt when holding Cristian, with the added thrill at now being a granddad as well as an uncle. As I say, I am very grateful to still be alive.

As my health slowly returned in the months and years following 2007, the process I have highlighted began of accessing, remembering, understanding and then articulating a lifetime of emerging theory that had been applied in practice. The foundational core of that thinking was summarised in the series of diagrams I am showing you. After my energy also slowly returned, I was then able to revisit each.

All are about belonging and their potential application in design practice. As energy spans grew longer, more files and boxes of drawings in my archive shed were explored, with items assembled that might be helpful. I was now in what I saw as 'extra time', with every moment being precious. You may have not only known equivalent experiences, yours may have been far worse, with acutely painful, even disabling, consequences. I do not know. If you have, do receive a big hug of understanding and support from me through these pages.

I am also aware of how privileged we are in the UK. In an earlier era, I would have died. Just as I would not then be able to write as I am, it may even be that you would not be reading what is written. Yet, by writing and reading, we are both now very much alive! As a result, there is a sense in which we are all in 'extra time', as one of the most privileged generations ever to have lived. Some may not have realised that is the case, but I know that I have. My further privilege has then been to be grateful before my life does end, when it would be too late.

Contrast my own growing awareness of vulnerability with one that, as an example, many young men can easily feel, which is of being 'indestructible'. I do not think I ever thought that specifically of myself. Nevertheless, I am sure that the sense of being physically vulnerable was somewhat distant in my early years. I now see knowing of my vulnerability as being another privilege. For, it is a reality for all of us in life.

One further benefit of that pivotal experience in 2007 is that I am increasingly aware of how important it is to see life in a much bigger, more detailed as well as real context. This is not least because my health failed because a small detail within me – a gland – almost ceased to function, with so much energy then lost and an end then being in sight. I knew of a thyroid, but not much more. I am now very aware it makes thyroxine that is essential to human life. So much so that I now take a substitute every morning to make sure my body is fully served.

We all comprise many such parts. We are also all dependent upon each functioning. For, each is special and in a relationship with other parts, resulting in a body that can work astonishingly well. A thyroid is but one of many such parts. Specialists more learned than I will be able to explain the role that each performs, as well as how one part works with all the other parts of the body, thereby enabling someone like me to live.

Do then imagine:

a. Each part as a circle within the bigger and more complex three-as-one diagram, as in Image 28, that is me. Do then:

b. Look in a mirror and see the same sequence of circles overlapping as one in you as well.

As a result of that focal experience in 2007, another realisation was confirmed. For, I became even more aware that doctors were able to help me for one specific reason. It was because the component parts of my body were not only the same as those in my generation, they were also the same in generations before my own. Medical practitioners had learned lessons from health failures, as well as successes, in other people before – and even long before – my own era. As a result, one doctor told me:

'Ray, there are a lot of people walking around with the problem you had, but they do not realise it. There have also been many people in the past that had the same problem, without my colleagues knowing what the issue was. Many would have lived far longer if practitioners then knew what we know today. Indeed, many died unnecessarily.'

That then helped me realise:

a. That we are all, in a sense, made up of systems within systems, with each being a form of body-based ecosystem, as summarised in Image 29 and then in the diagram in Image 30;

b. That 'we' includes people from generations that go back in time. How far back? I did not initially know. I will come back to that in due course, as it is directly relevant to my quest here;

c. That throughout recorded history there appears to have been a consistency of parts-in-relationship-as-one in the components and construction of the human body. If that had not been the case, it would be impossible for one generation of practitioners to be of help to those in difficulty in succeeding generations. Just as:

d. Practitioners in my generation would also not be able to look back to insights gained in eras before and deem them to be of relevance now.

That realisation then helped me with another. It was that I now take seriously insights from the past, not just about the make-up of our bodies, but also the very make-up of life itself. For what we know now is built upon lessons learned long into the past, with consistencies they saw still applying today. Our response may be different, but the consistencies in bodily construction still apply. That recognition then enabled me to explore even more fully arenas known to generations often long before my own with a new form of affirmed confidence. This was, especially, when seeking answers to the core questions being asked here.

It was then that I began to be certain that the observation of parts-in-relationship-as-one life, as summarised in my core diagram, was evident in eras in the past as well as in our present. An implication then was that the same should apply in the future.

If that is not the case, no one could plan with any confidence for anything. If that is the case, the same consistency could also then be seen to apply at any point in recorded history, with consistent parts-in-relationship-as-one being evident in every context ever lived. All are then multiple parts that are in multiple relationships, so much so that they can be seen to be integral to one total, consistent and ongoing picture.

As a result, the whole of life had, for me, become a multi-dimensional sequence of inter-related three-as-one diagrams as a living, place-based and time-based totality. There was evidence of that being the case in the past, in the present and that can then be expected to be there on into the future.

As has been seen, the more I looked and observed over decades, the more I realised that none of these circles overlapping as one is separate from the other. All are part of a time flow of history that functions together as one in the place that is life on our Earth in our cosmos. With each new era, the total picture will vary, but the consistency in principle remains, with an astonishing sense of equally consistent continuum being the consequence.

If you think I am overstating this, do simply look around now and check back in the past. When I have done so, I have been amazed by the evident consistency.

As a specific, the more I looked, the more Diagram A in Image 29 seemed to apply in the present and in the past. Each combination of parts could be 'clothing' that was consistent with the lives of the people living within. That is why a realistic assumption was that the same diagram – and hence the same clothing – would also apply on into the future. That was especially when knowing that it is a future that holds the deadly serious predicament heading towards us all. If so, two further questions followed. They were:

. How far back does, what I began to call, the 'three-as-one diagram' apply?

And:

. How far back has that predicament been there that we all face now?

I did not initially know the answers to either of these questions. What I did know was that the history of humanity and of our Earth and cosmos had to be relevant to any understanding of what has happened since and is happening now. Such an understanding might then also be crucial to our response, as we all journey forward into an inevitably shared, as well as bleak, future.

When I first noted that three-as-one consistency, I was in my teens. That awareness then grew exponentially during my student days. It was as if I was looking through a window into a total approach to life. It was a way of seeing that needed to be understood. That was especially because my goal was to discern answers to a rising number of questions concerning the whole of life, of which we are all a part. It was a totality that was now in trouble and could come to an end.

It was also a totality that, for me and for you, was finite with a beginning at conception in our mothers' wombs. Again, I did not initially know what even that observation implied, when looking at life's bigger picture. All I could do, at the time, was make note.

After 2007, I was able to explore its implications in depth, with outcomes now being explored through these pages. For now, do simply note:

a. that any consistency within my body and yours exists and that it will have an end:

b. That end will come despite that consistency, it would seem, going back in time, generation before generation;

c. Despite medical knowledge being based on past understandings, to then be tested, added to and explored in ever greater depth in the years since and:

d. Despite the confidence gained along the way that enabled interventions in the health of so many in our present, with the expectation of healing and ongoing benefit in the future.

As you have seen, I did not know how far back that consistency went. What I did know was that I needed to know the answer to that question. For, my expectation was that it could give insight into answers to the big core question that I have tabled, which is 'Life, what on Earth is it all about?' This was especially when in the context of health failure and death. My expectation then became that any answer had to apply not only to life past and present, it also had to apply on into the future. Critically, that was if there was then to be a discerned reason why death frames life, so much so that it always seems to win.

Whatever those answers were, the consistency evident in a three-as-one diagram seemed to challenge, if not temporarily hold back, the inevitability of death. As a result, it seemed to be key to any prospect of any life being able to live at all. For, when there was a loss of that consistency, as in my thyroid failing, the whole of my body began to fail, with an end to my life being in sight. It would also now seem that the same principle applies to the failing well-being of our Earth. As a result, I will come back to the relevance of a three-as-one diagram more fully in due course.

For now, it is important to note that that consistency – or loss of it – appears to define the viability of everything that is alive. It also does so in any context. For, everything that works comprises component parts, whether personal or not, all of which operate in a multitude of relationships. Even when working, all are still framed by the prospect of not functioning, with an end to viability then being in prospect. I noted that when my Lambretta – and later my Mini – needed the help of Rita Dalrymple's husband!

There was then another intriguing prospect. It was that each three-as-one must have had some form of origin and a context that included its beginning. It then became apparent that no person, no place and literally no thing is outside of that consistency's total embrace. It is everywhere in every context, with each having within it contexts within contexts. All are then surrounded by more consistent equivalents to the three-as-one context and, it would seem, without limit.

A lot was happening, therefore, in my early student era, with insights gained that seemed to ripple on and on in the many years since. My agonised experience in 2007 then enabled me to look back at those younger days and gather together foundational observations. That, in turn, had another consequence. It confirmed for me that, in order to make more sense of my life here on planet Earth, it was necessary to commit time to understand more fully than ever before these ever-present phenomena. I had to explore with new rigour, the many layers of context that are within me and that surround me out into a seemingly limitless cosmos. I had to explore more fully the systems of parts in a relationship as one, which were already there inside who I am, as well as outward in this astonishing phenomenon that I was calling 'Life'.

In order to do that, I needed reliable information and not just speculative ideas.

For, the issues I was seeking to address were simply too final not to be taken very seriously. I had, therefore, to discern and work with certainties and not the opposite. I had known of this need for several decades before 2007 and had responded accordingly, but its necessity was now etched even more deeply into my life. Reliability not speculation. Certainties only, therefore, and not guesswork. I will say more in due course about how I established what I now deem to be a source of core information that I knew could generate the confidence I needed. I will do so as we journey forward Step by Step.

Before I go further here, do ask yourself the same question I asked myself, which was:

. How can I be certain about anything in life, when life is in the context of death?

When you ask that question of yourself, I suspect you will agree that a starting point must be an appreciation of how amazing life is. As a result, it is important that we seek to understand its reason why with care, as an expression of that appreciation. We must even do so when beginning to grasp how final and costly an end in death will be for each one of us as individuals. We must also do so when, at least, beginning to grasp the dire implications of losing the life of our Earth.

I trust you can begin to see why I have stressed both the sense of amazement and that of intrigue about life. For me, there had to then be a reliable reason for both feelings. That reason must be understood as we all face the prospect of our personal, as well as shared, beginning and end. It is only then that we can:

a. Make sense of our own lives and, from there, life itself here on Earth. It is also only then that:

b. There may be the possibility of reliable, as well as relevant, responses following.

Our own journey through these pages, Step by Step, is such a reality-based exploration. As you have seen, it will include my own response to the many issues being raised. You will then be able to test those conclusions against the life and death, as well as reality-based, criteria that you may also establish. All our well-beings may depend upon your, as well as my, response.

As you have seen:

a. At an early stage in my own journey, I knew that individual identity, relationships and a sense of belonging for people in a place were somehow key to answers to the big questions I was raising. Death then crushes each. As a result:

b. I also began to realise that the consistent design themes I was seeing in life were constantly endangered, so much so that failure and death were ever present and even inevitable everywhere. That observation was so evident that:

c. I knew that it had to be crucially relevant. That is if any world view explanation, as an answer to the question why, was to be credible.

One phrase that I re-examined during my recovery was my use of the verb 'to enable'. I then renewed my conviction that I, as a designer, cannot force or make people belong. I can, however, enable such a sense of belonging to be experienced by people in a place. The people involved can respond or not to that enabling possibility. They can do so by allowing the context that I can provide to influence who they are and how they relate to others. If, as a result, a sense of belonging for people in a place is seeded, that precious experience can then be nurtured, helped by the place. It can even be 'enabled' to grow. A consequence then can be that a positive relationship between people and the clothing of a place can also grow.

Part of that enabling process was also to 'enable' a context where the risk of failure in the fabric of the place was almost non-existent. For, that would give reassurance to the people living in the scheme. Realistically, doing so 100% was impossible, but minimising such risk was, nevertheless, a central goal. For that minimised risk to continue, a rigorous maintenance programme was always needed. Even then some form of degrading was always inevitable, such is the ever-present nature of decay leading to death in our world.

When I have spoken about 'enabling' using design skills, some of my contemporaries have challenged me by saying that role is too limiting. For, their view was that an Architect should be able to:

a. Self-express, with the design, in a sense, embodying his or her own identity and then:

b. Define outcomes for others by, in effect, telling them what they need.

I understand the rationale inside both of those propositions, but I do not accept their primacy. For, my own approach is not ultimately about me. It is to serve. That is why I deem being able to help others – and do so by enabling – as being a huge privilege. It is a privilege that I am grateful to have known on many occasions. In my latter years, I continue to see that privilege as my motivation in whatever years remain.

As you know, the seed of that conclusion about enabling a sense of belonging came when, as a young child, I observed the way my parents served others in their shop. Early in any conversation with a customer, they would say, 'How can

I help you?' I grew hearing those words. For, their goal was always to genuinely help others. As my parents' son, that is why my privilege is to help others by enabling. I then became a student who valued that approach, when preparing to serve others through my intended workplace as an Architect. During those studies, I then had the opportunity to focus my efforts on how I could perform that task of 'enabling' places where people could belong.

As you have also seen, an early insight came when noting the conception and birth of living beings. For, a baby starts as a seed that is fully him or her, but with the need for protection, nurture and growth. Hands on care is then needed when the child is born. It is also important that the mother and the midwife wait for the right moment for the baby to come forth.

The many consistencies in that process have, for me, led to techniques that can 'enable' a successful delivery of belonging-based design solutions for clients. The mere knowledge of techniques alone, no matter how well developed, does not, however, ensure success. They must be applied, understood and even lived in practice. There has also to be testing of the principles, with lessons learned, ideally before application when working with real life clients. For, as with designing and constructing a building, successful theory applied in practice does not 'just happen'. Hard work is involved.

I am pleased, as well as grateful, to report that I had such an opportunity, when at college to develop and apply theory in a rigorously tested context. I will say more as we journey forward. I will also show you how tested theory was then applied, with a well-used built outcome in the high profile, inner city context in South London that I have already mentioned. You will then see how that theory into practice sequence led to more examples all over the UK, with the thinking in each being rooted back to that college era student exercise. It was an exercise based on the principles that I am outlining here.

Allow me now to emphasise that buildings do not 'just happen', nor do their designs. Just as a baby does not simply appear. All have context and all involved people who are 'hands on'. As a result, schemes also do not suddenly appear on a sheet of paper, without a lot of thought and work. Nor do drawings become constructions, rising by themselves on building sites. Work is always needed. It must be work that is focused, managed and deliberate.

That may again seem obvious. But, once again, sadly, it is so obvious that it can be overlooked. I am highlighting it once more because the same principle applies in every arena of life. Do hold onto that observation. Do also test it yourself, because its crucial importance to our journey here will become clear in due course.

When focusing in a little more, the amount of time needed to design and construct a building can be substantial. From my experience, as I have suggested, that process starts with a context and what is called 'a brief', which sets out the purpose of the intended scheme. The design must meet the requirements set out in that brief. Those criteria are crucial to knowing whether what is designed and built is successful or not. The reference point is always the reason why for the project.

Indeed, often more time can be spent on understanding the context, in the formation of the brief and then the design process emanating from each, than the time needed to construct the actual building. As an insight, a building may take a year to construct, but the process leading up to site work can easily take three years. Larger projects can even take decades before foundations are dug. So crucial is that, often hidden, very deliberate and totally necessary pre-construction, preparatory stage. I am highlighting this again for three reasons:

a. It is to affirm the sense of intrigue that I began to feel concerning so many consistencies in life. I was not only observing them, I was also living them. I was doing so, initially, when at my drawing board as a student. I then explored their principles when with colleagues in my office. Whether with pencils, pens and paper or when working with computers, theory was being lived in practice:

b. It was again as if I was looking through a window into something far more, glimpsing something of the context and briefing stage that led to the consistencies I saw everywhere in life. I have used the word 'tantalising' previously and it was very appropriate. For, I could sense a form of life-preparation having occurred before our Earth and cosmos was constructed as a building that could be inhabited:

c. I am also highlighting the crucial preparatory stage, remembering one or two student colleagues who appeared to think schemes appeared on drawing boards and matured to viability all by themselves. That was judging by their inability to get on with the work in hand. Failure was then staring at them full face.

Do have that last parallel in mind as we prepare to discern:

a. The reason why for life and, from there:

b. The brief and the scale of preparatory work necessary before life's conception and birth and hence before our amazing planetary home could be constructed. Do then:

c. Imagine the foresight, care and discipline that had to be applied to enable the equivalent of drawings and specifications to be prepared before the scheme that is Life could be built;

d. Do then anticipate the scale and depth of detail needed to build a 'Ray' or any other living being, set in the context of the multitude of life support systems essential for any of us to live;

e. Do also see that information being encapsulated in the DNA, not only of everything that lives, but also for the whole of cosmic as well as Earthly life.

For, hundreds of skilled people can often be involved in the pre-construction preparatory process, so that, what can then be, many thousands of other people can know what to build. Do then note that I know of no practitioner who deliberately designed and built a building that was not to be safe as a viable place in which people can live. Just as I know of no car designer that deliberately built a car that was not safe for its occupants. The same principle applies to aircraft and fridges, just as it does to food products and many other aspects of everyday life.

A lack of safety can then reflect a lack of understanding or an inadequacy in care. Often, when a product is designed to harm, it is in the context of conflict. Again, the implications of that observation will become evident as we journey forward.

For myself, my goal has always been to build positives and not negatives. It has been to enable new life to be born, using design and construction processes. Each step then requires the care shown by a mum protecting and nurturing her to-be-born and new-born child.

The comparison between my work and that of a mum and a child being born, to then grow toward maturity, adds to the sense of privilege I feel as an 'enabling' design practitioner. For, in many ways, I see my role as being a form of midwife. The equivalents of mother and a child are then the people and the places that I have sought to serve, with my focus being a sense of belonging. It has been with safety that enables life to live as a priority, fully knowing how ever present is the risk of failure, harm and even death.

With that affirmation of the primacy of enabling a sense of belonging as a backcloth, allow me now to go back, once again, to my early diagrams in Images 23 to 29, to then go forward when learning about ping pong balls.

Heading Eight

PING PONG BALLS

Image 33: Three ping pong balls, with all touching

When first observing and then exploring the 2-D diagrams I have shown you, a further source of intrigue was the 3-D Diagram C in Image 29. That was because that arrangement was possible, not just as a drawing on a sheet of paper. It could also be seen physically in actual three dimensions and in a form that could be looked at from many angles and be touched. More even than that, the content of a drawn diagram could be held in my hands, just as it can be in yours.

For, as part of what my tutors at the Architectural Association School of Architecture saw as an awakening exercise to help students see the world around them afresh, we were asked to do something that was unexpected. With all my first student year of new-found friends, I was asked to go out and buy a box of ping pong balls.

We were initially not told why. That became evident when we returned and started a series of exercises, using those ping pong balls. They started with a question. It was whether each ball was the same size and the same spherical shape. Our answer was 'yes'.

We were then told to imagine each ball as a volume that could be assembled with other ping pong balls, all of which we now knew were the same in size and shape. I suspect the sense of intrigue I began to feel was also there for all my student colleagues. This was, not least, because there was a certain smile on our tutor's face. For, he knew what we were soon to discover and, I suspect, those findings intrigued him as much as they would us.

As part of a studio journey of discovery, he then asked each one of us as individuals – and hence not with others – to carry out a series of exercises by gluing one ball to another. I will say a little about each shortly. When I do so, once again, do note that the principle of consistency was tangibly there in every dimension of what, for me, became foundational exercises. This was not least because every student came to the same conclusion.

All the ping pong balls were the same size. All were also fully spherical. I later learned that anyone anywhere in the world will then find that a sphere holds the most efficient and compact volume. When anticipating the exercises that follow, could I suggest that, if you have not already done so, you may find it helpful to buy a box of ping pong balls and carry out the same exercises?

You may then find that the outcomes we discovered those five-plus decades ago to be as intriguing as I did, and tantalisingly so.

The first exercise was to find out what was the maximum number of ping pong balls that can all touch each other, when laid out on a flat surface. If you do get a box of ping pong balls, do try it yourself, just as I have on several occasions in the years since. I am certain that you will find that the answer will always be three, as in the photograph of a recent exercise in Image 33 that introduces this Heading Eight. All my fellow students came to the same conclusion, as I expect you will.

I then noted that there was a correlation with the diagrams in Images 27 and 28, as well as Diagram A in Image 29.

In a second exercise, we were asked to establish the maximum number of ping pong balls that can touch one central ball. Once again, all had to be on a flat surface. The answer was always six around the one central ball, as in the photograph in Image 34. The total number of ping pong balls in that cluster is then seven.

Do then note the resultant 3-D model echoes Diagram B in Image 29. Again, do try the exercise yourself and see if you come to the same conclusion.

When I did the exercise, I noted that, in many cultures, a week comprises seven days. In several, six days in the week are for work, with one day for rest. The logic behind this format is that the one day of rest provides an opportunity for reflection on the working week before and preparation for the working week to come. That set-aside day then benefits the other six by enabling a sense of cohesion, as well as refreshment, for all seven days.

Image 34: Six ping pong balls with all touching on central ball

There was a sense in which both Diagram B in Image 29 and the 3-D model using seven ping pong balls were both saying the same thing. It was a form of geometric consistency. It was also one that others in many cultures may have noted and even responded to in their daily and weekly lives. That consistency was so evident that I remember clearly the sense of intrigue I have mentioned being heightened. My eyes were being opened.

Once again, it was as if I was also touching more than just ping pong balls and the geometry of spheres representing volumes, fascinating though that was. It was then as if I was physically handling something that was already there, engrained in the very structure of life. It was so 'already there' that many people long before me had been able to discover the same astonishing consistency.

As a result, I realised that, in our own era, my student year was but the most recent of a long line of intrigued discoverers. So much so that generations before our own had made their rhythm of work and rest consistent with a 2-D and 3-D geometry. They did so, it would seem, because they knew that structure was already there in life. As a result, a six to one format is there today in a seven-day week, accepted and used by billions of people around our globe.

The sense of intrigue did not stop there. The last exercise we were asked to carry out took the single layer arrangement of six around one a huge step further. For, we were asked to see how many ping pong balls could be assembled around one, not just in two but in three dimensions. It was, therefore, with all the outer balls touching a central ball. I cannot remember the expression on my tutor's face when he made that request. The reason was that I was, by then, too intent on finding out the answer myself.

We all started with six balls around one on a flat surface. I then added three, as in Image 33, above, with another three-as-one added below. All the encompassing ping pong balls then touched the one now almost fully hidden in the middle. There was also no room for any more balls. As a result, there was only one answer to the question:

. How many ping pong balls can surround one in 3-D, with each touching the middle ball?

For every student, that answer was always the same. It was twelve. With the ball in the middle, the total was also always thirteen. It was not only impossible for any more balls to be added, all the twelve outer balls touched the central one central ball, now hidden within. Do relate that conclusion to Diagram C in Image 29.

Do also note that the shape of the ball in the middle is then echoed in the overall shape of the twelve balls clustered around. You can see what I mean from the photograph in Image 35.

Image 35: Twelve ping pong balls around a central ball

The sense of intrigue that was already rising, then grew even more when I noted the following:

a. The twelve surrounding balls comprise a series of four groups of three-as-one and that:

b. Each cluster of three is then on the side of the central ball, as well as above and below.

My mind soon began to race. For, I had grown knowing of north, south, east and west as 'four corners', as an interpretation of our world. It was as if the cluster of 4 x 3 ping pong balls around one was saying, wherever we look and wherever we go – north, south, east or west – there is always a three-as-one. What that then meant, I did not initially know. What I did know was that there was a consistency. For, just as the weekly structure of six days around one can be seen in a geometry that is already there in life for all to see, so there was another consistency apparent in the very structure of the way we perceived our world.

In both contexts, there was a three-as-one focused on one, whether that is 2 x 3 making six or 4 x 3 making twelve. Once again, I did not know where this was leading, but it was very intriguing, to say the least.

That very tentative, but almost magnetic, observation then took on a new dimension when attending an early lecture on how to make a building stable and not fall over. I am sure you will agree that it is important in the design of a place for people!

For, having noted three-as-one as a foundational geometry that could be discovered anywhere around our world to be already there in life, that observation suddenly took on a whole new meaning. That lecture was given by another tutor, this time on building structures. His role was to press home how important it is for students to know that every building must be, what is called, 'triangulated'. For, if it is not, the building is not only at risk of falling over. It could also collapse, with people being hurt, perhaps fatally.

Imagine a stool with one leg. It cannot stand by itself and will immediately fall over. Then imagine that same stool with two legs, with both legs being of the same size. It will probably hover for a few moments, but still fall over. Add a third leg of the same size and something special happens. It will remain standing. That is what my lecturer in structures meant by 'triangulation'. Three legs lead to stability, when two legs and one leg do not.

The same principle applies when a human being sits on a one-legged stool, with both of his or her two legs down. The outcome is a structural triangulation, with that arrangement also being stable. Do try sitting on a one-legged chair yourself, without putting either of your legs down. You will quickly see the practicality of the lesson being taught. Do then put one leg down and follow the sequence, arriving at reliable stability when both of your legs have triangulated with your one-legged stool.

Even if you are on the opposite side of the globe, structural triangulation will apply. It is a fact in life, no matter who you are, where you are. Just as three-as-one ping pong balls is a fact that can be discovered everywhere. You will see an example of a triangulation in the three-legged stool in Image 36.

Image 36: Triangulation in a three-legged stool

When expecting that principle applying anywhere on Earth today, my expectation then became that it had always applied in the past. I then noted the buildings illustrated in lectures on the history of cultures around our world. All seemed to recognise the need to triangulate by constructing walls at right angles to each other or, say, in the form of buttresses. All were applications of the need to triangulate, with the goal of making an otherwise unstable structure stable. My assumption then became that that principle should continue in the future. Indeed, the lecturer also assumed the same, as his goal was that his students designed and built structures that would not fall over!

If that was the case, the principle of triangulation could then continue even to the end of life here on Earth. Indeed, I even wondered whether its application may be relevant to how that end will come. It was, however, far too early in my thinking process to come to any considered view. I did, however, start to wonder how far back in the past the necessity of triangulation had also applied. For, one implication was that it has always applied and has done so as a pivotal part of life's DNA.

Thanks to the explanation given by a lecturer in building structures, triangulation is very evidently highly practical. It is there in the design and the way we sit on a stool. What is then called 'structural triangulation' can prevent even the largest and tallest buildings falling over. If that format was not built into a design, its structure could move and become a parallelogram, with collapse then being in prospect. If that happened, the building would not only be unusable, tragically, people could also get hurt and even die.

It was when realising that risk that the privilege of serving others by designing places took on a necessary heightened degree of personal responsibility. It was an awareness that has grown and grown in the decades since, as I have sought to convert college-based theory into nitty gritty constructed practice. For, if my design is structurally wrong, people could die. Part of not getting it wrong, as a result, had to be to get it right. A way of doing that was by applying the principle of triangulation.

In order to demonstrate the scale and extent of the relevance of triangulation, our structures lecturer pointed to the steel frame of an office building that was under construction, as well as others when complete. An example is in Image 37. He asked us to note what is also called cross bracing, where triangles are formed with steel girders.

I will show you other examples shortly of this very necessary principle being applied in practice. For now, could I ask you to note one resultant dimension that is fundamental in my own discipline of Architecture? It is also directly relevant to some colleagues having stressed the need to self-express through their design work.

Image 37: John Hancock Center

It is that an Architect must embrace and obey laws that include structural geometries that are already there in life. Some are so fundamental, that if we try to live as if they did not exist, people could die. Do have that serious insight in mind as we journey forward. Do also look out for other examples of triangulation in life, as we explore more fully a context for:

a. Why it is that life exists in the form that it does here on Earth?

b. Why is it that life always seems to be vulnerable to death?

Then add to that:

c. Why is it that, if the principle of triangulation is not applied to a building, it could become an agent of death?

As I learned about inherent geometries in life that need to be there in building structures, it was, once again, as if each is evidence of something that was far more. It is a 'something' and a 'far more' that were very much already there in the whole of life. It is a 'something far more' that was also already there in human relationships. That three-as-one, as well as the structural principle in triangulation, then seemed to apply in practical ways in every arena of life. It was still early days. My question then was why?

Allow me now to focus a little more on that theme.

As I absorbed the lessons being taught, it was then that I noted afresh the way we human beings continue from generation to generation. It is when a mum and a dad conceive a child to then be born. Each is then part of a relational three-as-one. Indeed, it is because two can become as one that we all exist. As a result, life lives and can continue because of a form of relational triangulation. Even in that context, it began to seem that that geometric structure was not only already there, everywhere, in life, it also had to be there for life to be able to live. It is as practical as any form of structural triangulation that enables longevity in buildings.

In both contexts, it is a three-as-one that is so already there that anyone can discover and work with it, anywhere in the world. Indeed, if we do not then live within its framework, life could die, with living beings becoming extinct.

In my mum and dad's context, my mum was special as Jessie. My dad was also special as Norman. My parents longed to have a child and, hence, to use that geometric term, they longed to 'triangulate'. They were having difficulties. That longing was known to close friends, who knew of a girl who was pregnant with a child. An unwanted child was then welcomed into my parents' lives through adoption. Two-as-one then became three-as-one. I can only but imagine the joy bursting within my mum and dad, so deep had been the longing they had felt. What was then extra special was that triangulation enabled my parents to triangulate even further, when I was conceived and subsequently born.

My parents' lives, my sister's life and my life have all existed because of the principles inherent in the geometry of a triangle and, hence, in triangulation. It is a fact of life that is universally evident in ping pong balls, just as it also is in stools, steel girders and in office buildings. Once again, a great deal more on this anon, because the implications of this very consistent observation are nothing less than huge.

At this point in our journey, do simply note this foundational insight in my own process of discerning theory and applying it in design practice. For, I was seeing the practicality of the design relationship between a geometrical structure in a building and the relationships shared by precious people well known to me. It was a recognition of a consistency that was already there in the design of material places and in the design of people. It was a fact that was already there in life, waiting to be discovered and then articulated. It was also a fact of life that I had not expected as an outcome when buying a box of ping pong balls!

I do not know why my tutor smiled when he introduced his class to those exercises. My suspicion is that he was also amazed by the geometries his students were soon to discover. I also do not know whether he had seen the connection between structural triangulation and clusters of ping pong balls. My suspicion is that he had. Had he also seen the design relationship between building structures and family relationships? I suspect not, but I may be wrong.

Had other students also been amazed? My answer is 'yes'. This was not least because one had noted a triangular format in the reproductive organs of human beings. We then saw the same in the relationship between two eyes and a nose, as well as two nostrils and a mouth, with two ears adding to a series of triangulations that help us to see, hear and even smell the world around us. Our head and shoulders follow the same triangular principle, with two arms and hands then enabling us to triangulate and pick up objects. Even the science of locating objects is called trigonometry, which is based on an accuracy only possible when having three points of reference.

What I have yet to find, however, is anyone from my era that has noted the correlation between human relationships and those shared by cross braced girders and spheres when they are glued together. If you know someone who has, do let me know. I would like to compare notes.

It was as a result of those formative exercises, that geometries were added to my early diagrams as key insights into my emerging understanding of life. Each pointed to positive, life enabling design relationships, focused on belonging between people and places. I now knew that there was, not only an inherent consistency already there in people, I was also beginning to see it in the geometric 'building blocks' of places. So much so that I knew that I was onto something that was special and tantalisingly so. That awareness then led to another reason for my growing sense of intrigue.

For, when looking again at the twelve ping pong balls around one, as in Image 35, I noted that the central ball is always the point of reference, whilst also almost visually disappearing. It is consistently there, but not easily seen. What can be seen is that central ball's spherical shape echoed in the way the twelve ping pong balls gather around. It is as if the life of the central ball then lives in the life of its many neighbours.

If you do glue twelve around one, you will then find that, together, they have become a single entity that can be picked up and enjoyed in 3-D. You should even be able to hold that twelve around one cluster in your hand. As a result, any notion of some balls being above, whilst others are below and around, becomes secondary to that single formation. All the enveloping balls are not only:

a. A series of three as one relationship, they:

b. All have a focus that is inward to their shared point of reference. Every ball is then:

c. A component in all the resulting geometries and:

d. Shares a consistent, almost family-like, identity with every other ball, so much so that:

e. They can all be seen to be as-one.

That 'so much so' is so specific and tangible that it is like holding the Earth in one's hand. When doing so, it is also as if that 'Earth' is then looking outward, implying the ability for every ball and every spherical relationship to relate to even more. It is then as if that Earth not only knows it is being seen and held, it is also as if we are all referencing far, far more. That scenario and that prospect are then possible because of that central ball. For:

a. Just as twelve ping pong balls can be added;

b. So can a potentially unlimited number more, with:

c. Everyone being in a consistent relationship, whilst also:

d. Having a single point of reference in the central ball, layer by layer.

For, every ball will always be in a design relationship with the central ball, even when the relationship of the outer layers is via the first. That first cluster of twelve then become initiators as well as, in a sense, intermediaries, with that first ball not only as the consistent point of reference. Its identity also indwells the identity of everything that then follows.

What I then found to be fascinating was that no matter how many other balls

– possibly hundreds – are subsequently added, the same geometrical principles of three-as-one, triangulation and a shared geometric point of reference always apply.

I would like to think that each of my student colleagues was as amazed as I was. Just as I would also like to think that our tutor's smile reflected an equivalent excitement, when knowing that something seemingly non-consequential could enter the realm of the exceptional.

Some may be thinking, 'This is a lot to see after buying a box of ping pong balls. They are, after all, only ping pong balls.'

I understand that, but that is part of my point. The seemingly ordinary can also be seen to be extraordinary. As a result, what can be seen to be everyday is also worthy of much closer examination. From there, what may seem obvious should never be overlooked. For me, it was then by not overlooking that my spiral-in journey accelerated with consequences that became pivotal, life changing and with answers to all the questions being raised then being within reach.

An interesting sequence of exercises had, therefore, transformed to become, for me, a window into an ever bigger and an ever more consistent insight into the already-there structure of this amazing phenomenon that is life. It is a life that includes, not only who I am and who you are as relationship-based unique people, it also includes the very fabric of the world around and within us.

On several occasions in the years since, I have bought other boxes of ping pong balls, wondering whether the same principles still apply. They have every time I carried out the same exercises. If you buy a box and experiment yourself, I am confident that your own exercises will come to the same conclusions. To make sure, on one occasion, I used golf balls. I needed stronger glue, but the outcome was, once again, consistently the same!

You may be in Beijing when you read this, or you may be in Mumbai. Wherever you are, if all balls are the same size and spherical, I am certain of the outcome. None of us can go back centuries and millennia in time, but my solid expectation is that the conclusions will still apply, with the same consistency. I will say more in due course, but my suspicion is that some of our forebears did go out to their equivalent of a shop selling their own version of ping pong balls. My expectation is that they too may have carried out a similar sequence of exercises.

For, when looking at well-known structures such as the Parthenon and the Pyramids, it became clear that their designers and constructors were well versed in triangulation. Not only are triangles used as a design form, the very fact that the buildings have stood for many centuries point to its structural implications being applied as theory and with the goal of very long-term practice.

. Had they too learned using their own version of ping pong balls?

I do not know. If you do, please let me know. Having shared that, as an example, I am convinced that our forebears in the medieval era in Western Europe, including here in the UK, did know and I will explain why in a future Step. For, its implications in terms of questions answered are as vast as they are profound.

When I first assembled my own ping pong balls, I was indeed amazed, just as I have been in the decades since. As I write, on the shelf opposite my desk is one such cluster of twelve ping pong balls around one. It is there because I now know that what that cluster represents is even more amazing than the outcomes of exercises when using them. Once again, more on that anon. For now, do simply note that they hold the key to how life can live, without the constraint of an end in death.

In those student days, I began to think that the geometries I was discovering are, in a sense, design theory that has already been successfully outworked in built and usable practice. Not only were built structures proof of that being the case, so was every structure in life itself. It is theory that is, as a result, tested and seen to be very practical. Indeed, if it is not consistently applied, not only will failure follow, but so can the ultimate failure in an end that is death. Relate that localised prospect to our global predicament here on Earth and I trust you can see why my own sense of intrigue kept growing. It not only grew as I explored the geometries before me, it was also as I sought answers to the huge questions that I was beginning to raise.

As a result:

. Could a lack of triangulation, say in the ecological dimensions of life, be a reason why many are now beginning to say that our Earth is in such trouble that it may soon be uninhabitable and even die?

. If the answer is potentially 'yes', could it be that we have been denying an intrinsic, even structural rationale in life, so much so that final failure is on the way?

I did not know the answers initially because the prospect of 'yes' to both questions was so huge that I found it difficult to grasp the implications. Some fifty years on, I now have a clear insight with many answers following. When I look back, I am then aware that even pondering those questions enabled me to begin, what became, a long-term process. Its focus was whether hidden design principles inherent in life, including geometries, could be relevant not only:

a. To the construction of every dimension of life, but also include:

b. The very reason why life is as it is and with the seeming inevitability of death.

That process then led me to ask:

. Could those geometries not only enable access to an answer to the question why, could they, in turn, help me in a working life when designing places as clothes that fit the lives of people?

In my early student years, I could not be certain. I was, nevertheless, more and more intrigued and ever more tantalisingly so.

What then became a further source of intrigue was another notion that, as you know, I had begun exploring. It was that those geometries were like design letters in a language that was already there, written within life. It was a language that then enabled the equivalent of words, sentences, paragraphs and even books to be written. It was a language made of volumes, such as those within spheres, as well as a multitude of parts that were all, in some way, in relationship together as one. Depart from the consistency within each and difficulties came, with the outcome being failure, leading to death. The geometries that I was discovering were then part of that design language in life.

Thanks to my tutors, my eyes were, indeed, being opened to see a world that already existed. Indeed, it was a world that had done so long before my own era. That longevity then implied that the consistency I was seeing would continue to exist in the future. Whatever their implications, those 'hidden', as well as fundamental, 'geometries', had to become an essential context for my own intended work as an Architect. For, I had not invented them. They were already there. Their existence was as certain as anything was certain in life. That certainty had been there in the past, to be there in the present. I could then confidently assume that it would be there in the future.

As a result, a key phrase then rose to the fore. I have now used it on several occasions. That phrase is:

ALREADY THERE

Heading Nine

ALREADY THERE

Image 38: Light passing through a prism

A series of diagrams, a number of exercises using ping pong balls, alongside lectures that highlighted fundamental structural principles in life – all were pointing to a consistency in life that had been already there in the present and in the past. The assumption then was that they would continue to be 'already there' on into the future. They will do so whilst there is time. It may even be that a breakdown in that consistency is a factor in the Earth now being seen to be such trouble that it is dying.

One consequence of that already being there was that each consistency could be discovered, seen and articulated. Each was, therefore, inherent in life. Each then contributed to a framework that enabled life to live. So much so that if they were denied, the outcomes could almost certainly be negative and even deadly. It may then be that those death-based outcomes could be discovered, articulated and potentially addressed and even remedied, with negatives then becoming positives.

That principle of 'already there' then helped me see that there is another related dimension to life, focused on my own work as a designer of places. It was as if there could be solutions already there to problems that were also already there. Those solutions were not only potentially in the minds of colleagues in a design studio, but potentially everywhere in life itself. If that was even remotely the case, I felt a sense of excitement as well as a sadness. For, somehow, that intrinsic dimension had been lost from general view, other than when we try to sit on a stool or seek to make a building stand up and not collapse.

It was as if there was a dynamic to life that was akin to a language that could be accessed, understood and articulated. It was a language that could even access solutions. That language could be sought and known, but perhaps very few people knew that it even existed.

Nevertheless, it was as if that language was also, somehow, alive. For me, it felt like a wave that was out there and that could be surfed. I did not fully understand what I was thinking. It was the glimmer of a notion and a sensation that held a certain expectancy, with a touch of excitement. I did not know why that language was there, but I was increasingly confident that it existed. Five decades later, I now know far more, so much so that:

a. I have included a surfer holding a surfboard on the front cover and:

b. I have set out my subsequent journey exploring questions and the practicalities of the answers since received. It is a journey that also:

c. Tells of my attempts to ride that wave.

As a result of that sensing and discovery of a language in life, another sequence of questions arose that I thought might even point to their own answers. They were:

. Was that already-there language saying something?

Followed by:

. Was that already-there language also saying something about the reason why life on our Earth and in our cosmos is as it is?

And then, with that feeling of tantalised excitement rising once again:

. If I listened carefully, would I be able to hear what it was saying?

If I did hear:

. Could that language reveal the answer to the ultimate question why?

When those questions first came, once again, I hardly knew what I was thinking. Nevertheless, the seed of a further insight had been sown. It was one that would bear substantial life-changing fruit in the years that followed. Once again, I will say a lot more as we journey forward. In the meantime, I trust you can sense the expectancy that I had begun to feel.

For, when still as that longish-haired student, I had begun to explore what was, for me, a new and deeply intriguing possibility. It was that the language I was beginning to see might, not only enable access to the answer to the biggest question of all. It may also articulate a way of seeing our world. Crucially, it may do so from the perspective of the answer to the big question 'why?'. If so, the implications were potentially as highly focused as they were vast for all of life, in its many dimensions.

Do specifically note that it was a language that was visual, geometric and about a multitude of parts in a vast array of relationships. None of its words were written in English. Nevertheless, people anywhere in our world could read and articulate each using an always-contemporary, shared language. That is what I was in the process of doing. In the midst, I was, in a sense, not just articulating, but also seeking to translate, the original language I was discerning was already there.

I also increasingly knew that, somehow, it was speaking. It was even speaking to me. More and more questions came forth, with each one inter-connected. Many were nuanced amplifications of others. They were then almost a form of a dialogue that I was having with myself and, perhaps, something that was also far more:

. Could that inherent language hold the key to a world view of theory that outworked in very evidence-based design practice?

I began to think 'yes'.

. Could its consistency also be key to my goal of enabling a sense of belonging for people in places on a wide range of scales and in an ever-enlarging range of contexts?

Another 'yes' came. As a result:

. Could that design language enable me to hear and see whatever reason there must be for life being as it is?

. Could it enable me to help others see and hear it as well?

. Could it even help others to know the very reason why life exists?

I then wondered whether an ever deeper and wider understanding of that language could enable a response to two other questions, which were:

. Could that language and the reason for life inherent in it then inform every aspect of the way I live and, indeed, the way we all live?

. Could it even be key to the way we respond to our own inevitable demise, as well as now the deadly serious predicament that has been my point of reference through these pages?

It was not long before I began to give a name to that possible way of thinking, communicating and even designing. As you know, the term I used was:

THE DESIGN LANGUAGE OF LIFE

Once again, I will come back to its huge implications as we journey forward. For, I later became 100% certain that it held the key to every answer to every question that I have asked and could ever ask. In the meantime, yet a further source of intrigue began to surface.

For, I had noted that language carries opportunities for expression, with content and implied meanings. It can also summarise and enable access to what many have called 'truths'. They are insights that can be difficult to access without the words and sentences that a written as well as spoken language provides. Yet more nuanced, as well as penetrating, questions then became relevant:

. Could the design language of life specifically have as its focus 'truth' about what life is all about?

. Could it also be an expression of that ultimate reason why?

. Could it then enable access to what is 'true' about that reason why?

. Could it even enable an insight into where that 'truth' originates?

When writing that sequence of questions, I am again very aware that I have used the words 'true' and 'truth'. I have done so when knowing that both have been contested and even fought over across the millennia by many people all around our world. I felt it necessary to bring them to the fore and do so as my intended point of reference as we journey forward Step by Step. For, if they have any meaning, I concluded that they must be relevant to the huge issues I am seeking to face and respond to through these pages.

When first realising this possible connection, I soon learned a key lesson. It was that, in order to discern and work with the design language of life, not only was a lot more understanding needed, it was probable that I would have to make very specific changes to my current thought processes. That change may also have to include my vocabulary of words and sentences, as well as their meanings. For, I was increasingly aware that a new arena was in the process of opening-up before me. It was also huge. I had, therefore, to somehow be able to access and even live its contents.

As a result, I once again knew that such a change could require the realigning and redefining of my own way of seeing the world. Crucially, that would also include the very way that I think. It was then that a new realisation hit hard. It was how close was the way I think to my understanding of who I am. It was as if changing my thought processes required a change in the 'me' that is me! I will be open with you and say that, initially, I found the prospect as frightening as it was challenging and exciting.

I can remember the moment when I first began to see the necessity of such a change. It was early in my college days, with diagrams being formulated in my head. I was riding my Lambretta 125cc scooter when I came to the brow of the very steep Lances Hill in my home city of Southampton. Looking down, I knew that I had to leave the safety of the essentially horizontal road I had just been driving along. I had either to not go forward or to take a risk by pointing my scooter down the hill. I knew that I was not indestructible. I also knew that going forward was likely to be reasonably safe. The risk was, therefore, not about being physically hurt. It was not being able to turn around once I started my descent. As I trust will become evident, I concluded to descend, as well as even accelerate down the hill, albeit with caution and care.

Taking that parallel and applying it to the prospect of a need to change the way I thought, I concluded to go forward, aware of its potentially life changing implications. Indeed, my life was then never quite the same again. For, I knew that I was now on a definite journey with a destination, still undefined, in mind. It was one that would and did have inevitable twists and turns, as well as ups and downs, with many potential difficulties ahead. Yet, I had taken a risk and I knew it.

Picture again, me holding a surfboard. I had dared to change from one way of thinking – equivalent to unchallenging calm water – to another that could be tumultuous. It was from one thought process that was known to one that was fundamentally unknown. Yet, I knew that the 'waves' ahead were already waiting to be surfed. There was even the sense in which each was saying:

'Come on in. You will fall off, but you will get back up again and the ride will be well worth while.'

I did not realise it at the time, but when I look back, I am aware that I had already begun to surf, almost without me knowing. What was now different was that the change was happening with my full knowledge. I knew that I was on my scooter equivalent going downhill. I could even feel it happening. It was not only from one way of thinking. It was also from one way of living to another. Crucially, it was to one that could potentially make sense of every aspect of everything that is. Some fifty years later, my surf-riding journey continues, with many theory-into-practice lessons learned from a life lived in between. I have fallen off my surfboard many times, to then clamber back on again. There are, I am sure, also many more occasions yet to come.

At this point, allow me to pause. For, I want to thank you again for sharing in my journey so far through these pages. Thank you, therefore, for reading thus far and, in a sense, listening to me talking. If you have joined in with your own questions, answers and equivalent exercises, I am grateful that you have felt able to do so. It may then be that we are both beginning to ride our own respective waves, as well as scooters downhill.

As with your life's journey, mine has embraced all my other smaller journeys, including that of being a design practitioner. In my 72 years of life, my own bigger picture has involved reading many books on an ever-widening variety of topics, as well as absorbing an enormous amount of information through newspapers, magazines, newscasts, and television and radio programmes. I have attended many courses and lectures, as well as participated in many conversations, discussions and debates. Emails have also flowed back and forth with friends and colleagues in abundance. All have in some way influenced:

a. My thought processes;

b. The way I see our world and, from there;

c. The designs carried out by teams working with me.

Hidden within each of those projects are the diagrams and 3-D ping pong ball clusters you have seen. Each embodies theoretical ideas. Each is also an insight into me riding the wave that was my realisation that there is a design language in life. Just as a wave can get bigger, so can an insight into the meaning of that design language. As a result, there are several more words and sentences, which I will soon explore.

For now, allow me to share some more analogies and with outcomes. Do then see each as an ongoing part of a spiralling-in journey toward the answer to the huge core questions that I have raised. They concern why life is as it is and, hence, its reason for being. Do then, once again, also see each as a hand opening even further in order to catch a ball that is the answer to the question 'why?'.

A prism and a thesis conclusion

Do look again at the image that introduces this heading. It is of light passing through a prism. When doing so it changes from being white to being multi-coloured.

As you have seen, analogies are important to me. I have used several as insights, but there is another reason. It is because each exists and, I have concluded, each does so as an articulated insight into life's reason why.

A surfer and a wave are visual. Riding a wave can be anticipated and felt. There is then another analogy that is equally visual and that can also be felt. It points to the fact that each of the diagrams and insights, as well as design projects I am describing, are but 'the tip of an iceberg'. For, what is seen is merely visible evidence of far more that is unseen.

I am very aware that my life is but a tiny, above water, part of an iceberg that is life's much bigger picture. Indeed, my understanding is that the whole of life – with its many people, its multitude of places and its seemingly limitless number of parts and relationships – is like a vast iceberg, with what is unseen below the surface being far bigger than what can be seen above. Yet what can be seen above is totally dependent upon what is unseen below. If what is below shrinks, then what is above becomes even smaller.

I have told you of the occasion when I pointed 'the scooter' that was my life downhill, with an inability to return to my starting place. It was during that ongoing journey that I became aware of the core answer to the questions I have asked, focused on 'why'. It was then that I also realised that there was an originating source that held the answer to that question. It was hidden, but I had sensed it, as well as felt its presence. More even than that, I had begun to see it, albeit through what some people have called 'a glass darkly'. I was aware that what I was seeing had shape. It also had an identity. Without knowing the detail, it was the originator of the design language that was already there in life. But I did not know what it was saying. I did, however, conclude that that 'originator' could be telling me the answer to my core question why.

With that thought as a backdrop, I also began to realise that, not only the answer, but also the identity of the source of that answer, could be known. One implication was then specific. It was that that source had made it possible for there to be a question in the first place. For, that source had seeded in life the ability for me and you to ask questions, including ones starting with 'why?' All such questions then had as their focus the desire to know as much as we can about why life is as it is.

As a result, to be able and even to be allowed to ask questions was another window not just into the answer to the question why. It also enabled a form of glimpse of the identity of the originating source. One consequence of that notion is that every question that can be asked has as its root both the identity of that source, as well as its reason why for life existing at all. I, therefore, found myself needing to know the identity of the source that I increasingly knew was already there, but that I did not know.

A further consequence was that:

a. The reason for a wave analogy and:

b. The reason why I could attempt to ride it and:

c. The reason why an iceberg is small above the surface, but much larger beneath and:

d. The reason why mums and dads can birth children and:

e. The reason for parts-in-relationship-as one and amazing geometries that are intrinsic to life.

All are there because of that originating source and its own reason why. All are a window enabling a glimpse of that source's identity and purposes. Indeed, even the ability to glimpse and ask questions seemed to suggest that the identity of the source was accessible. It was even as if that source wanted to be known.

It was soon after that very intriguing possibility dawned that something happened that was beyond amazing. I will now use another deliberate analogy, as illustrated in the photograph that introduces this heading in Image 38. What happened was as if the 'light' of my life, which included my theory applied work, seemed to pass through a form of 'prism'. I have previously mentioned an occasion when I was momentarily dazzled, unable to speak. More specifically, those moments were so filled with light, that was all I could see. It happened in the spring of 1970.

That led to the beginning of a dramatic change in my understanding of life, as well as my thought processes. For, the change that I knew was necessary then began to happen in a way that was as totally unexpected as it was overwhelming. My spiralling-in journey had reached its destination and I saw the source that I knew was already there waiting. I saw the 'something far more' that had allowed me to sense and then anticipate it being already there. I had discovered the originator of the language of life, with one consequence. It may now be possible to hear from that source, the answer to my core question why.

I will have to keep using analogous parallels, because the experiences that I am now seeking to describe are almost beyond description. Indeed, that is why analogies can be helpful. They can point to realms that could not otherwise be accessible. For one outcome of that experience was that I am now certain that the whole of life is 'a window', akin to a 'taste' or 'glimpse', of that something more.

When taking the prism comparison one step further, what I was then able to see, thanks to that change, took on an even more 'colourful' dimension. It was as the core insights that I had already noted emerged on the other side. A totally unexpected, dramatic change had occurred. White light became many colours, with each with having an impact on what I was beginning to see as the design relationship between people and places.

That relationship now embraced another. It was that 'something far more'.

It was that 'source for the whole of life'. It was also the one that 'originated'. Each of those terms were helpful, but each was also in danger of feeling too mechanistic and cold. A different word or phrase was needed that, somehow, also told of the heartbeat in life that I had sensed and I now knew was already there. I had previously used the term 'the life essence'. The name now had to be more specific.

As you know, I saw that 'life essence' being at the generic centre of my spiral diagrams. That 'life essence' then permeated the lives of people and places, as well as everything that lives in every place. That permeation also includes the multitude of life support systems needed for all life to live. Even then, before the spring of 1970, I did not know what or, notionally perhaps, who, 'the life essence' was. What I did know was that it was living in the clothes that are life, just like the central ping pong ball in my sequence of clusters. The design shape of life then told of its shape within. At the heart of that shape was a three-as-one, which was an astonishing conclusion, but it was self-evident. More than that I did not know. Another question had, by then, come. It was:

. Would I ever know what 'the life essence' was?

I knew that such an outcome was possible, but when it came, it was as much a surprise for me as it was overwhelmingly new. It was also as tangible as it was specific. As a result, it could be described, embraced and explored, as well as understood with increasing clarity. Even then, I realised that there was always far more.

As a result, that prismatic experience:

a. Informed everything that then followed, to become:

b. An integral part of my life that also:

c. Enabled me to anticipate an ever deeper understanding of an all-embracing theory about life that could be outworked in design practice, with then:

d. The prospect of a consistency between my life's work designing places for people and the context that led to the brief that, in turn, led to the biggest project of all: the whole of life: past, present and future.

In the years since that prismatic moment, as a team member in many design processes, I have been constantly learning. I have also been slowly changing, with a growing ability to live what I now know to be the core reason why for everything that is life. I have a long way still to go. Writing these pages is, therefore for me, part of that ongoing, as well as life changing and life growing, process.

You may now, very understandably, be asking:

. What was that prismatic, life changing experience?

. Am I also saying that each design project can have an equivalent prismatic dimension?

Do allow me now to apologise. For, I must hold back and say that I will answer both of those questions as we continue our journey forward. My purpose now is to set as full a context as I can, whilst pointing toward what is still to come.

With that in mind, please do stay with me. For, the experience I am referring to is, to use another analogy, the foundation on which so much more will be able to be built. It is the reason for 'the wave'. It is also the reason why there is 'an iceberg above and more below the water' in the very first place. It is, indeed, 'a prismatic' way of living. It is also a way of seeing through 'a window' to the source of the answer to every positive question 'why?'.

Allow me first now briefly to go back to that downhill scooter experience on a steep hill in Southampton and sketch other insights. For, one thing is certain. It is that I held onto my handlebars very tightly and did not let go. I did so as soon as I decided to go forward and take a risk. I also did so when knowing that there was no prospect of a return. I then had no choice but to keep going.

At this point, do imagine how the next few moments felt. For, my trust is that the significance of 'holding tight whilst taking an irreversible risk' will become very evident as we continue our journey forward. Its relevancy will then not only be in relation to my own life, with its inevitable end. It will also embrace the global tragedy that is now unfolding as the predicament we all face becomes increasingly real. It will even enable a resolution of the contradiction between:

a. The desire to belong that we all, in some measure, have here on Earth, whilst:

b. At the same time knowing that we are all facing an end to life on this our endangered planetary home.

I suspect we have all had prism-like experiences, after which life was never the same. My much later near-death experience in 2007 was, for me, another. Nevertheless, even that was secondary to the one from my scooter-riding days. Indeed, that more recent experience was fully embraced by the first. One outcome then became certain. It was that, when prism-like events occur, a new and enriched way of seeing, thinking and acting can often follow.

One of my reasons, therefore, for mentioning some of mine is so that you may also remember your own.

I am also using various analogies with that same goal. It is to provide a context for your own parallel ways of assessing and sharing your experiences, with the insights you have gained then being tabled. These pages are one of my ways of sharing. There will be other ways that are appropriate for you. I am looking forward to seeing how you do so and to then learn and grow. It may also be that the way you share will become part of THE BIG DEBATE that I am advocating, as a response to THE BIGGEST CHALLENGE we are all facing. As you know, if that happens I would be pleased.

For, there is one further certainty. It is not only that we all think, at times in similar, yet also in divergent ways, it is also that we do so using varying images and, often, different languages. In addition, we all have insights that are valuable, with the consequence that we all need to listen and learn from each other. It just may be then that there can be a shared language and an equally shared way of thinking that we can all access and use. You may already know of the design language that I have noted.

You may already be fluent in understanding and using it. You may know of another language that is also inherent in life. If so, please do table it.

Heading Ten

ALREADY HAPPENING

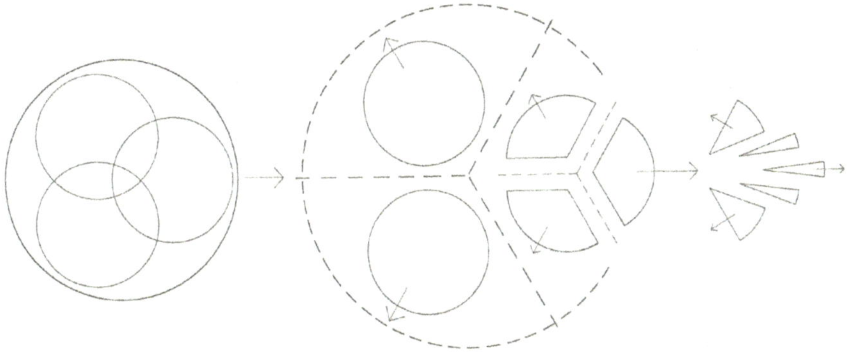

Image 39: A breakdown diagram

Allow me now to spiral-in further to tell you a little more about another prismatic experience. I have already highlighted it, but a further insight is now timely as we spiral-in and as a hand gets even more ready to catch the ball. It is foundational here and occurred when I was still a student. It was a harsh reality that, when it hit, was overwhelming and utterly life changing.

Its implications have then shaped and rippled through these pages, with implications that are as vast as they are directly relevant to us all. I will now give you a little more insight into how that realisation came about. It was that the Earth is dying.

As I have suggested, there is a sense in which there is an ultimate context for every other context imaginable in life. It is, as a result, also the ultimate prospect that must be addressed. That is, if together we are to urgently shape a way of thinking, with positive actions following. I am not referring to 'the life essence' here, but the issue that it may be able to resolve. How? I did not initially know.

You already know a summary of the issue that I am referring to. My awareness of it started with observations of life, followed by diagrams and exercises using ping pong balls. That sequence was explored during my student years when studying Architecture. As those studies approached their climax, I had to write a Finals thesis. In it, I was required to explore fundamental issues about what was, at the time, often called 'man and his environment'. By 'man', it meant everyone, whether male or female. By 'environment', everything else in life was then embraced, including other living beings and life support systems. The link phrase 'and his' then told of the relationship between the two.

As you have seen, for me, that phrase was in the process of changing to become 'the design relationship between people and places', with places having a living dimension.

I was aware that my thesis might be able to set the scene for my life's work as an Architect. I, therefore, concluded to look at the effect of buildings, as well as other engineered structures, on the lives of people. My goal was to be able to consolidate, as well as understand, more fully my still formative diagram-based exploratory thinking. My focus was by then my further goal of enabling a sense of belonging and doing so through the design of places.

As a detail, the written thesis followed completion of a Finals design thesis, which was a prototype: 'Meeting Place', specifically designed with that goal of enabling a sense of belonging as its reason for being. I will say more about that in Step Two. A key point to note now is that my journey toward outcomes of theory in design practice had commenced when my written research work began.

My course at the Architectural Association started in 1966. As part of my Finals research, I read a report published by 'The Ecologist' magazine in 1972. It was a Penguin Book entitled *A Blueprint for Survival* that has since been reprinted on several occasions. As you can see from Image 40, on its front cover was a quotation from *The Sunday Times*.

The pivotal word, 'Survival', is very stark, as well as precise, in its meaning. For the writer, that word implied one thing. If we do not sustain the habitat that enables life to live on our planet, we will not only know failure, we will all also die.

To use an understated cricketing term, the scale and the breadth of the issues raised 'hit me for six'. To use

Image 40: The front cover of *A Blueprint for Survival*

another from surfing, the effect on me was 'wipe out'. As a result, that quotation then applied to me, for 'nothing' has been the same since. That was, not least, because I had, by then, realised that death was already there in life. That fact came to the fore shortly before. It was when I had learned of my dad's terminal illness. It would now seem that the same outcome applied to the whole of life. That is, unless we human beings did something about it.

As I prepared my written thesis, the more I pondered the implications of 'survival', the more its reality began to impact everything that was me up to that point. I could see only one core conclusion. As you have seen, I have repeatedly called it the predicament we all face. Its significance is there in the title of the Penguin book. For, my conclusion was simple and direct. It was that:

'THE EARTH IS DYING'

I remember vividly the moment that realisation first dawned. I have touched on it before. It was one that was prismatic in the extreme. It was also spring when I wrote those concluding words. At the time, I was much the same age as the young man holding my sister's babe in Image 31. My student home was a small room in a Stockwell flat in South London. I had the use of part of a windowless basement as my workplace.

When I reached my conclusion I could go no further. I stopped and put my pen down. I stood up and left my desk, to navigate the darkness of the basement. I opened its door and ascended stairs out into what was a fresh and sunny day. I looked up as birds around me sang and daffodils welcomed life into their world. It was then that the impact of my conclusion fully registered. It was then that a second heart-breaking realisation came. It was that:

'ONE DAY THERE WILL NOT BE ANOTHER SPRING'

As you know, tears rose and fell uncontrollably, as they have on many occasions in the decades since. They have done so when I have explored, in much greater depth, the implications of that prospect. Increasingly, it was when knowing that those consequences encompassed every human being, as well as a myriad of other creatures, inhabiting this finely tuned 'building' that is our Earth. Even when restrained, those tears now indwell each of my remaining days. They have also motivated and helped reshape so much of my thinking and, from there, my actions.

Perhaps inevitably, my responses have been inadequate to the magnitude of the predicament now known and the task we all face. As I have shared, when I look back, I am very aware that everything I have thought and done, since those very stark and prismatic moments, have fallen short of what I could and should have done.

Once again, I must apologise for that falling short.

Even when recognising and being open about that failure, my expectation is that my best – and indeed all our 'bests' – will, nevertheless, all end in the same, which is failure. For, tragically, humanity may succeed in part, but my expectancy is that we will not be able to fully resolve the dilemma we are facing. It would also seem that that issue has been there for centuries and even for millennia. With the scale of the tragedy being vast.

Some have suggested, as I have, that death is integral to life. What was new for me in my student days was that an end in non-viability could occur soon and it could be global. What was ahead for my dad, despite the help of so many terrific and highly skilled medical teams, was now in prospect for every human being, as well as every creature, alive on this our home planet. That includes me.

The predicament headlined in a book by *The Ecologist* magazine in 1972, having been there for a long time, was already there waiting to be seen. Indeed, it was almost like another iceberg below water, waiting for the Titanic that is life. An Earth, that many thought to be unsinkable, was now sinking. It was also as if a wave coming toward us is so big that no one could ever ride it, with the prospect of no one ever being able to surf again.

In the past, many people have recognised that death was part of life, but some saw it as part of a process that was progressing forward. Death was, as a result, part of a cycle that either repeated itself or that had a trajectory that was upward. Many Architects have held an ascendant view. Yet, as the implications of 'The Earth is dying' register, it is becoming clear that there may be no future into which to progress, never mind ascend.

As a result, there was another dimension to the contradiction that I have highlighted between belonging and death. It is between world view expectations and reality, so much so that I will explore it in much greater depth as we journey forward into STEP TWO.

As you now know well, in 2007 my health failed and I could have died, with me now being in 'extra time'. When I wrote an early draft of these paragraphs, it was Tuesday, September 12th, 2017. On a Sunday, I try to read at least two national newspapers. The Sunday before was, therefore, September 10th, when, on that occasion, I read a copy of *The Sunday Times* and *The Observer.*

Image 41 hosts the headline in the Science and Technology supplement of *The Observer.* On its inside page was a timeline in decades setting out a journey toward the end of life on Earth. I have included the headline in order to reaffirm that its harsh prospect is now very fully in the public arena in the year that I now write, 2020.

On that same occasion in 2017, I also watched a BBC2 programme entitled *The Search for a New Earth.* As with 'survival' in the *Ecologist* magazine, that BBC title summarised the direction of its content. An extract from the 'Critic's Choice' accompanying the television schedule of the *i* newspaper, dated September 11th, 2017, then explained a little further. It is also in Image 41 and is as stark as that in *The Ecologist* publication. The impact of both was then made even more real when I noted who had proposed that we should search for a new cosmic home.

It was Professor Stephen Hawking, who was perhaps one of the most esteemed scientists of our modern era. He was facing the end of his own life, having lived much longer than was first expected. His life had been extended over decades, thanks to a huge array of technical and personal help. As a result, he understood the effort needed to enable his own 'extra time', since being first diagnosed with a terminal problem in his college years. It would also seem that he understood the seriousness of his own diagnosis for life on our Earth.

Do then read the headline from *The Observer* supplement and the Critic's Choice summary in Image 41 and do so together.

As you can see, Professor Hawking's view was that humanity has only 100 years in which to find and populate another planetary home. He had, therefore, come to the same fundamental conclusion as my own, more naively, decades before. He had also gone much further and given a specific time frame. My own conclusion was with comparatively little information. His followed a lifetime of observation and careful consideration. My short four concluding words in my Finals written thesis were by a student studying Architecture. His conclusion was in the final stages of his long academic and science research-based life. I was at the beginning of my life's work and he was at the pinnacle toward the end of his. His conclusion was then, like mine, as simple as it was tragic.

The diagnosis given by my dad's doctors, pointed to him having two years to live. I am grateful to say that he lived for four. As a result, he was able to be there when Jenny and I married in October 1974. Professor Hawking's prediction is more rounded, but equally as finite, with an end to viability coming toward us. My dad's latter months were traumatic, just as I suspect the latter years of life here on Earth will be, but the end will still come.

Stephen Hawking is now one of many who have realised the urgency of our global predicament. Many are also now searching for a new cosmic home, including such men as leading technology entrepreneur Elon Musk with, for example, his SpaceX programme.

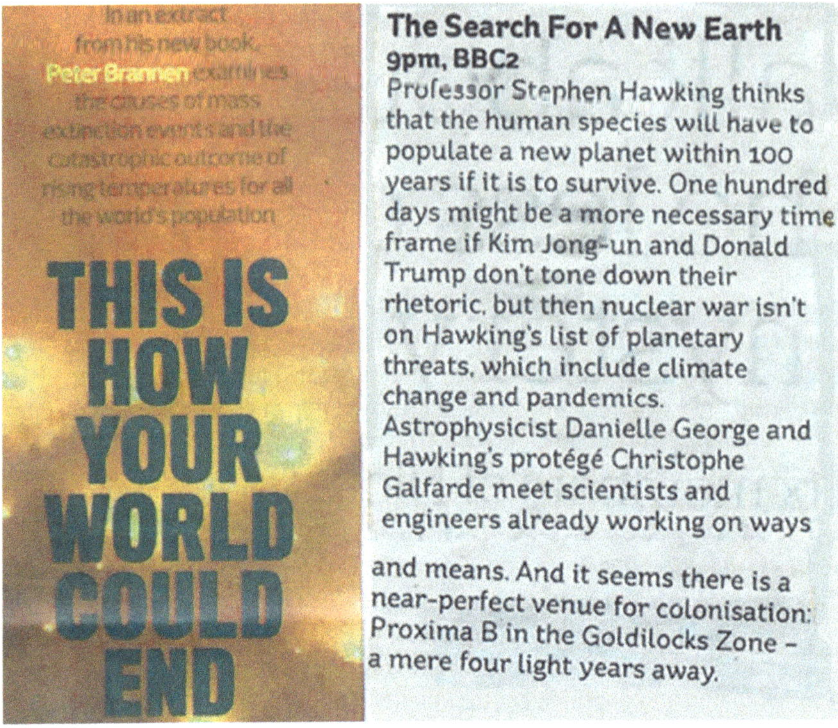

In an extract from his new book, Peter Brannen examines the causes of mass extinction events and the catastrophic outcome of rising temperatures for all the world's population

THIS IS HOW YOUR WORLD COULD END

The Search For A New Earth
9pm, BBC2
Professor Stephen Hawking thinks that the human species will have to populate a new planet within 100 years if it is to survive. One hundred days might be a more necessary time frame if Kim Jong-un and Donald Trump don't tone down their rhetoric, but then nuclear war isn't on Hawking's list of planetary threats, which include climate change and pandemics. Astrophysicist Danielle George and Hawking's protégé Christophe Galfarde meet scientists and engineers already working on ways and means. And it seems there is a near-perfect venue for colonisation: Proxima B in the Goldilocks Zone – a mere four light years away.

Image 41: The headline in *The Observer*, 10.09.2017 & the Critic's Choice summary of 11.10.2017

As a relevant detail, I noted reference in the media to a possible cosmic venue that is 'a mere four light years away'. I found myself being vague about 'a light year', so I looked up its definition. I now know that a light year is a measure of distance, calculated by using the speed of light as experienced here on Earth. I tried to work out how far a SpaceX rocket would have to travel over four light years. I learned that, in a vacuum and hence with minimal friction and hindrance, light travels at 300,000 kilometres per second. I then tried to work out what the distance would be to that cosmic venue.

If I am right, it is:

4 years x 365 days x 24 hours x 60 minutes x 60 seconds x 300,000 kilometres

At that point, my calculator quickly ran out of capacity. I, therefore, looked up a definition of a light year on Wikipedia, which was much simpler. There, I noted that a light year in distance is 6 trillion miles, which, when multiplied by 4, makes 24 trillion miles. Another calculation there suggested that such a distance would take 17,000 x 4 years for a human being to travel, when using a

Voyager 1 spacecraft. I also noted that human beings are unable to travel faster than the speed of light.

. How long would that same distance take a SpaceX craft?

I do not know. Elon Musk should. Whatever the time distance, it is almost beyond vast. As a result, my own life span and that of any astronaut will almost certainly only be the tiniest of drips in its ocean-like pond. Unless I am missing something and without in any way wanting to be flippant, it seems that some form of 'Doctor Who' time travel will be needed. That is, if human beings are to leave our Earth and find an alternative home that is, even then, only notionally viable elsewhere in the cosmos. Indeed, that may be the only way that such huge and, for me, almost incomprehensible, distances can be related to, when referencing the need to enable humanity's survival.

As far as I am aware, such time travel facility does not exist. Do let me know if it does. Indeed, do tell everyone you know. For, time is running short.

As recently as July 12th in 2020, there was a short article in *The Sunday Times* by Christina Lamb in which she reports the following:

'A number of wealthy entrepreneurs have ... entered into the arena of colonising Mars. Elon Musk, the billionaire founder of SpaceX, launched US astronauts into space in May and plans to establish a colony of a million people there by 2050.'

She then goes on to suggest:

'It's an extreme way to escape Covid-19, but in the absence of a vaccine, and with cruises off the agenda for the moment, he may have some takers.'

Her last comment might be tongue-in-cheek, but the article summarises the reality of the situation highlighted by *A Blueprint for Survival* in 1972 and by Professor Hawking shortly before he died. Our predicament is deadly serious, solutions are being sought and we are running out of time.

Even if there is another viable location, our predicament remains the same. It is that the life supporting ecosystems within our planet are experiencing a rapid decline, leading to non-viability. I mentioned this recently to a gathering of soon-to-be-qualified architectural students and did so as a context for their own professional lives. The response was obvious concern. One student sought to be helpful by suggesting the Earth might survive, even if humanity does not.

In response, I shared with him my observation that we can live when all of the other systems also live. They then do so as our support. If we must leave our Earth, it is because what remains of those systems is in such decline that we cannot survive. There is but one core implication. It is that many, if not most, of those life enabling systems have, by then, already almost ceased – if not actually ceased – to function. We will, as a result, not only be leaving an endangered planet, our Earth may have already become non-repairable. Even its own very robust resilience will, by then, have been overwhelmed and with no robust prospect of revival.

There is often mention of a tipping point, after which our Earth's life sustaining systems cannot recover. My expectation is that some advocates of space colonisation have concluded that such a tipping point has already passed. Add in the fact that space travel is currently available only for a tiny number of well-prepared people and at huge cost. The goal of five million people inhabiting Mars by 2050 is then ambitious, to say the least. I then looked up two statistics in order to understand that goal more specifically. The first was the current population of a city I know well, London in the UK?

The answer via Google is 9,304,000 in 2020. The colony proposed on Mars is, therefore, approaching half the size of London, which is a city that can function only when serviced, not just by the immense capability of the United Kingdom, but also because it is a global city that can access a global resource. If that multi-layered and extensive support system failed, London would fail. If the Earth's support systems have already failed, logically, five million people on Mars are in trouble.

If that target was achieved, a second statistic was the anticipated population of the Earth in 2050?

Again, using Google, one calculation is 9,700,000,000 or 9.7 billion people. Even if Elon Musk succeeds and a colony of 5,000,000 people, that is .0005% of the then global population, with a lot of people left behind on a dying planet. As a result:

a. Even Elon Musk's ambitious proposal leads to a deadly serious scenario, the magnitude of which is almost beyond comprehension. Despite that:

b. Its hard-edged reality must be faced and urgently so.

That is why the title of this book and its direction of travel are so explicit. That is not only because what is before us is real, it is also because we must all seek answers and know what to do and, crucially, do so when knowing why we are in the predicament.

As you saw, I felt peace in 2007, when I knew that I could die. This was in stark contrast to how I felt in my student days when first realising the magnitude of the dilemma we all face. I felt no peace, only the opposite in anguish and sadness. For, I realised we were all part of a tragedy of immense proportions. Not only did tears well up and fall then, they have, as you know, done so on several occasions since. On some, my body has shuddered, when realising afresh the implications of what lies ahead.

This has been especially when knowing that, if Professor Hawking is right, the process that is leading to an end is now moving rapidly toward its climax. I will, therefore, say it again. I am now an ageing man. My years remaining are small, but my children have decades ahead of them. Even if an end is delayed, they will see its implications long before. My recently received gift of a grandchild will also see the same. For, the demise of viability in our Earth's life supporting systems will almost certainly be fully evident in their lifetime.

As a result, the predicament we all face impacts the ones we love now and in the future. That impact is already registering and evidently so simply by reading newspapers, as well as listening to local as well as world news.

With that deeply tragic prospect very much in mind, allow me now to highlight another key contradiction in the way we often see our world. I have already pointed toward it, but more is now needed as we move toward the end of the first Step in our journey together.

It is a proposal that has influenced, at times very overtly, my arenas of Architecture and Planning and has done so throughout my lifetime. It is a way of seeing our world that has undergirded and even dominated thinking in Europe, as well as other parts of what many call 'the Western World'. It is a way of seeing our flow of history as human beings, set in the context of the history of our Earth and cosmos. It is one that now, at this stage in our journey, needs to be noted. For, it is a world view that assumes ascendancy, not only in terms of a past-to-present-to-future direction, but also almost as a human expectation and even a human right.

That assumption is then that the whole of life has moved from chaos to order, from the simple to the complex and from a form of 'darkness' to 'light'. That sequence, as an idea, was founded on the notion, not just of progress, but also of one that goes much further. For, it is progress that changes the very structure of living beings, so much so that one kind of living being becomes another, with each change leading to an increased ability to survive. The generator that leads to those enhancements is then seen to be fundamental in every aspect of life, not only on our Earth, but also in our cosmos. That driver is 'survival', which appears credible.

If ever there was a time when its theory must be tested in practice, it is now.

For, if it is 'true', then a change into something else that is relevant to our dire circumstance is needed of colossal proportions around our world. If it is not, then a more credible way of seeing our world is needed and urgently so. To change will also not be easy. Indeed, my expectation is that it will be traumatic, as so much needs to be re-thought. For, the assumption of a flow of history that is ascending has been in many minds for millennia. It became especially dominant in the 19th Century here in the UK. It then influenced expectations around our world and especially in Europe and North America as the 20th Century arrived. For, many thought the new era ahead of 100 years could host the climax of history.

. What would that climax in history be?

It was expected to be very different to the one concluded in the newspaper articles I have just highlighted here. Indeed, it was to be the complete opposite. It would be a climax, when we human beings had shaped a world that was without the tears that I have shed. It was a world, therefore, without pain and any form of negative breakdown. What was deemed by its adherents to be within reach was a social, economic, political and technologically based future that was harmonious. It was a future that, in a sense, would be lived in a way that was fully consistent with my core three-as-one diagram in Images 28 and 29. It would be one in which people would reach their full capability, unhindered.

When doing so, a perfect life on Earth would come into being. For, what was anticipated was an ascendant climax in a utopia – and I can identify with the heartbeat in many of the people that longed for such an outcome.

The key to enabling that prospect was a world view. It was based on, what were thought to be, certainties. Those certainties were grounded in what were also thought to be evidence based, scientifically framed, principles not only about life's flow of history, but also about the very structure of, as well as mechanisms in, life itself. Some people had even worked out how they could vary those structures and mechanisms in order to bring into being their own definition of a utopian perfection. Many also thought that Architects and Planners would play leading roles in making that transformation happen.

As we all know, with deep gratitude, the 20th Century did host remarkable transformations in health care and working practices in many countries and around our world. The lives of billions of people living on our planetary home have improved markedly. Yet at the same time, that century also hosted two world wars on a scale – and with a degree of devastation and cruelty – that many had previously thought to be impossible. As part of the carnage, hideous, at times genocidal atrocities were carried out in the name of a series of very defined views of how life could be structured. Each had as their goal a form of utopian outcome and each was designed to help bring that climax into being.

Many parts of our world have also been at war in the decades since. Along the way, the well-being of many people has improved, but none have become perfect. The physical environments in which they live have often also been significantly enhanced. Others are worse. No matter where and when, none could be called perfect.

Indeed, for many other people, as well as places, the outcome as we left the 20th Century was the opposite to the speculations that proved to be unrealistic on our entry into it. They were expectations that quickly led to so much pain. We are now in AD 2020. As we now move further into this 21st Century, a very different and more realistic, as well as evidence-based, expectation is now before us. It is not that of a utopia, supported by scientific projections. It is the opposite, based on actual and substantial evidence in practice from around our Earth. It is of a planetary home that will, in a definable future, not only not sustain life as we know it. It will also be a distinctly non-utopian world that is dying.

As a result, our forebears when entering the 20th Century could be shocked beyond measure to find that scientists, such as Professor Hawking, have been advising us to leave our Earth and colonise other locations in our cosmos. That sense of shock may be then exacerbated when knowing that the quite remarkable science-based entrepreneur, Elon Musk, is funding a process to enable a city half the size of London to be inhabited on Mars in 30 years from now. For, he is planning to build a place where a tiny proportion of humanity might start again, having left the opposite to a utopia. The implication then being that everyone else will remain and perish.

That is why, when revisiting my three-as-one diagrams, the variation in Image 39 became my way of describing what is happening. It introduces this heading and, because of its relevancy, it is reproduced again in Image 42.

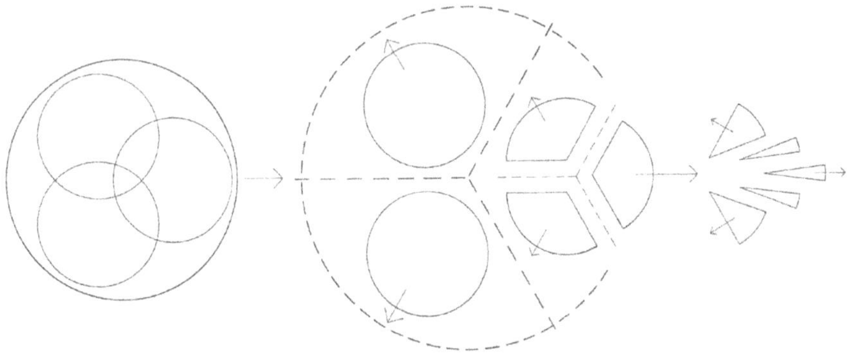

Image 42: My breakdown diagram

The harsh, even total, reality that it describes then leads to further crucial questions. They are;

. If that deadly serious prognosis is correct, why did people, especially, in the 19th Century here in the UK get it so wrong in terms of expectations and a world view?

Followed by:

. Have we learned from their mistakes to the degree now needed?

The answer to the second question would appear to be 'no'. For, although we are now increasingly aware that there is a problem, the response so far has been mixed. Dig a little more deeply and my observation is that the world view that led to the expectation of a utopia, as part of an ascendant view of history, remains dominant. Indeed, it is so entrenched that it is almost never questioned, never mind challenged. For, it is assumed to be scientifically and hence evidence based and, from there, true. If it is, even by my early and tentative definition of 'truth', it has to work in practice. As a result, another question comes to the fore. It is:

. Why are we now making our global situation worse, if the evidence in practice does not support the theory that led to that ascendant world view?

As a result, the 'science' that led to the theory is contradicting the 'science' now evident in outcomes in practice. Yet another sequence of questions then rises, which are:

. Is the earlier 'science' right?

. In the light of current evidence, should the earlier science-based world view be tested afresh?

. Is there something that should then be re-thought?

And even, when remembering one of my own analogies:

. Should our Western World and global community get ready for a prismatic change of both world view and thought processes on an enormous scale?

If the answer is 'yes', then we must all get ready for a steep, downhill mega 'scooter ride' of a lifetime and urgently so.

As you have seen, when seeking my own answers, I had to recognise my own role and my own failings. I suspect the same will also need to apply on a much broader base. For, we may all have to recognise when our thinking and our actions have been wrong. From personal experience, that will be far from easy. Indeed, it will be difficult as well as very painful.

For, I had to face the fact that the tragedy coming toward us is because I, with many others, had thought that a lesser form 'utopia' world was within reach. It may not be a perfect world, but it could mean a better lifestyle. Even an ever-better car, holiday and a redecorated home could be seen to be a part of a goal that has an ascendant, utopian flavour. Indeed, as I have intimated, my observations are that some people today even think that improvements are, to use my earlier phrase, a 'human right'. Once again, there have been times when I could be thought to be one.

The consequence has been more damage and more failure being inflicted on our global life support systems, as a result of individual attempts at fulfilling a variety of mini-utopian goals. This is a huge issue for, perhaps, us all, with enormous, as well as far reaching, implications. As can be seen, I am holding up a mirror with my face in it as I write. More on this anon, therefore. For now, do simply note the contradiction between any form of utopian goal and an Earth that is in deadly serious trouble.

With that in mind, there are then a series of underlying questions that also need to be asked. They reference something that may even be pivotal in the view of life that we hold. Those questions are:

. Why do we seem to want enhancement in life?

. Why are some people in such dire situations of poverty that their lives are endangered, whilst others are not?

. Are those extremes also intrinsic in life itself?

. Should we accept them, especially in the context of the global predicament we all now face?

And even:

. Should we try to address what some call gross and unacceptable inequality?

. Could that be a component of a much bigger strategic approach to the issues before us?

I will table my own answers to these and all the other questions that I have raised. I will do so as we journey forward, Step by Step. For each is important and must be addressed.

As we approach the end of this first Step, allow me to make one further observation. It is that many 19th and 20th Century world views led to varying forms of devastation. They include imperialism, fascism, socialism, communism and consumerism. In their own limited and focused way, they sought to address some of the questions I have raised. Many supporters would argue that theirs succeeded in part. Others might agree that each also failed in their core goals. Having been, on many occasions, a visitor on the socialist side of, what was known as, the Iron Curtain, as much industrially based environmental damage was inflicted there as in, say, the North of England during the empire era of the 19th Century. We are all having to live with the legacy from both in our modern era.

Huge effort went into both of those applications of theory into practice. As a result, yet more questions arise:

. Why did they not stop the environmental damage being inflicted?

. From there, why was it not possible to get it right?

As well as:

. Could this seemingly enormous, almost absolute predicament we now face, have then been avoided?

Then comes another question that carries with it some heartache, when looking back to the expectations held in the century now gone. It is relevant to the role my own professions were expected to have played. It is:

. Why did serious and let us assume well-meaning people in the 19th and 20th Centuries think that a utopia was within reach?

And then into our own century, when making it personal to me:

. Why, when wanting the best for the people I love, do I find myself contributing toward making our global position worse?

And even:

. Am I trapped in something that is unresolvable?

Indeed:

. Are we all, therefore, trapped in a situation that cannot have a positive outcome?

Professor Hawking's view was specific. We have, in the 21st century, to urgently plan, with a relatively short timeline, to leave a planet that will soon be unable to support life as we know it. I have also been open with you when saying that my generation is, in part, responsible for that anticipated need to leave. Just as, it would seem, is every generation before mine. I must accept and face that issue, just as I suspect we all have. The generation that succeeds mine is also in the process of making its contribution to the negative scenario before us. An even deeper question has then to be asked. It is:

. Is there something wrong, therefore, in every generation, so much so that we cannot stop ourselves making negative contributions to an already dire situation?

There is a sense in which that question requires each one of us to look inside who we are. When doing so, several other external, specific questions need to be asked. They are an extension to notional cosmic possibilities, already alluded to, that appear to be out of reach. They are:

. Not just generally, but where specifically in the cosmos can we go?

. I have heard mention of Proxima B in the Goldilocks Zone of the cosmos. Is it really an option?

. Assuming we can somehow overcome time distance issues, is that a suitable place where life, as we have known it here, could be possible?

Allow me to become steadily more focused, by asking once more a question that I have already started to answer. I am asking it again, so that you can table your own answer. It is:

. If there is somewhere, will everyone alive on planet Earth be able to travel to wherever it is?

Then comes the prospect of agonised decision making, which may even have to be taken by someone known to you. It is:

. If all cannot travel there, who stays behind?

An inevitable and highly contentious issue then follows, which can be summarised in two other questions, which are:

. Who makes those decisions?

. And how are those decisions made?

I have asked all those questions of myself over the five decades since my student days, as the timeline before us continues to shrink. The context is knowing of my own failure, a degree of selfishness in me and a resultant lack of care for others. With that critique in mind:

. Would I be qualified to make decisions that could affect the well-being of millions of others?

I think not. For, I have been and still am part of a problem that has not gone away. I have even made the situation worse, when wanting to do the opposite. It would seem likely that we have all done the same. In my own context:

. Did that realisation impact my own life and then my work and life?

. If so, have my thoughts and actions since helped or hindered life on planet Earth?

The last two questions are directed at me, just as they can be to every one of us. My own answer to those questions is to say that:

a. The way I have approached my life and work has helped ease the situation. Nevertheless, very sadly:

b. I have also contributed to our global predicament.

Really tough questions then return, focused on my own goals through my workplace. They are:

. How does my focus on enabling a sense of belonging by design affect our shared predicament?

. Are belonging and the proximity of death contradictory?

. Is belonging merely a nice notion that is irrelevant to our dire global situation?

. Is even love for others also irrelevant in the context of that predicament?

As a result, some may ask as a challenge:

. Are the seemingly 'soft' dimensions in life, including a sense of belonging, ultimately really in opposition to the 'hard' one of terminal decline in our global life support systems?

. Are both belonging and love, therefore, distractions that must be abandoned, so that we can all concentrate on an Earth in trouble?

My answer to the last question was as clear a 'no' as when I first asked it. That answer remains, with reasons that will, I trust, become clear as we journey forward. All these questions then lead to three fundamental issues that I had to face. Indeed, my suspicion is that we must all face them in some way.

The first is an expanded variation of the subtitle of this and all subsequent Steps. It is:

. If we human beings must leave our dying planetary home, what literally on Earth has life here been all about?

The second is:

. If I and we have, at least, contributed to the deadly serious predicament here, why do we think we will not do the same in the future, even on a venue in such a wonderfully named Goldilocks Zone?

And the third then follows, which is:

. Are we all, therefore, in a trap that may be of our own making?

Allow me now to emphasise the observation of a trap, by asking two more related questions. They are:

. Are we in a trap that we cannot exit?

. Are we in that trap because the reason for it being there is somehow inherent in what and who we are and, from there, what we think and do?

A good friend of mine often says that, when we meet someone we have not previously met, we should not ask, 'What do you do?' and hence 'what is your work?' His view is that we limit the person to a work role. Instead, we should want to know who the person is, when knowing that his or her identity is more than the work that they do. I have valued that suggestion, but my answer, rightly or wrongly, has been, 'What we do is an extension of who we are. The two cannot be separated. We can, therefore, glimpse who we are by what we do.' If there is substance to that response, then that last question rises almost to the top of what has become a long list. With slightly different phrasing, it is:

. Is the reason for the trap we are all in somehow inherent, not only in what we have done, but in who we are as human beings?

In the light of the seriousness of all these questions, I trust you can now more fully see why the subtitle of each Step is, 'Life, what on Earth is it all about?' As I trust has become evident, I chose it because:

a. Our situation is so dire that an answer is needed which is clear, substantial and one that must be respond head-on to the seeming facts we are all having to face:

b. I have done so, when knowing that a finger of blame must inevitably point at me, just as I suspect it will in some way point at all of us. For:

c. I have had to face my own failure in this serious context, just as, I suspect, we will all have to;

d. I have also placed the prospect of a dying Earth on the front cover, because my commitment to you is to be open about its primacy;

e. That commitment is, therefore, to face its implications for me as well as for you;

f. It is to do that despite my own failure;

g. It is also to do that because I think I have answers that I have come to see, albeit through a 'glass darkly', to be of value;

h. I have also tested those answers as theory and in practice sufficiently to be quietly confident that my conclusions, so far, are worth sharing. That is because:

i. Those answers do appear to fundamentally work in practice, with so much more still to learn and with many future lessons then being able to be explored and outworked.

The insights that I am exploring will, therefore, inevitably be inadequate and limited. Nevertheless, my trust is that they may point to a way of accessing and understanding far more. They may even begin an ever-larger process of defining a framework for answers to these and other enormous questions. Part of that ongoing exploration is also the proposal that we should all respond to what appears to be an inevitable end to viable life here on Earth.

We should do so by anticipating the huge traumas yet to be faced as that end approaches. It is when knowing that, if in even the smallest of ways, there are true successes in amongst many tears, the outcome will be worthwhile. For, it could be both extra time and a degree of meaning lived, perhaps, as never before.

I know that facing personal, as well as now global, death can lead to anguish, sorrow and tears. I do not want to be the cause of such pain, nor do I want to accentuate that prospect, but I know death will come. From my experience, it is unavoidable as we all seek a way forward that works in both theory and in practice.

Having shared that, you may have already concluded that I have been the cause of pain. If so, please again accept my apologies. For, I am very aware that I have taken a huge risk by writing as I have. If I may say so, you have also taken a risk by reading thus far. Nevertheless, if the insights tabled enable you to offer your thoughts, I would be pleased as well as grateful. It just may then be that, together, we may be able to help others offer their responses. If that happens, even more practical, albeit possibly at times painfully wrought, positive solutions may follow.

If that then leads to A BIG DEBATE in response to THE BIGGEST CHALLENGE ever to face humanity, my gratitude would be beyond measure. For we may all then, as a local and global community, seek out and even live an ever-deeper sense of purpose, whilst there is time. For, I am sure there is still enough of that precious commodity here on the planet we have all been privileged to call home.

So that you are aware, as we journey forward in future Steps, I will explore the following:

a. How I interpreted in practice the insights I shared about belonging, summarised in a series of diagrams;

b. How those diagrams then helped me establish the basis for what I began to think is the beginning of a way of seeing our world that works;

c. How that emerging world view then informed my life's work as a designer of places;

d. How that ongoing experience helped me define very practical tools that we can all use if our shared core goal is the same, and crucially:

e. How that way of seeing, how that theory outworked in practice and how those tools are, for me at least, directly relevant to the dire predicaments that we all now face.

I will also tell you more about the light of my own life going through that unexpected prism in 1970. It was indeed truly pivotal. In this focused spiralling-in and this ever-enlarging spiralling-out process, there will also be many more design schemes as examples of theory outworked in exploratory practice. Once again, do assess each in the context of two key questions that have been my point of reference. They are:

LIFE, WHAT ON EARTH IS IT ALL ABOUT?

And:

IF LIFE IS IN THE CONTEXT OF DEATH, WHAT ON EARTH IS IT ALL ABOUT?

When I have shared with you my own answers to those huge questions, another then follows. It is focused and is:

. Does each scheme contribute, albeit inadequately, towards fulfilling that answer to the question, even knowing that everything will die?

My own answer is a careful and grateful 'yes', but yours may be different. You may not even be able to give an answer. Indeed, it may be so difficult, that you may dismiss the whole exercise as an impossibility and hence of no value. If that happens, I accept that outcome and with thanks for even considering the question.

Allow me now to conclude this Step One by saying that I am very aware of the magnitude of the task before me. I am also aware of another factor that should be brought into play. It is that a sense of belonging is, in part, subjective and hence can only be experienced in the privacy of an individual life. As a result, a source of belonging for one person may not be a source of belonging for another. We see that in music and in sport, as two immediate examples. We also see it in a different way in my family belonging being mine, just as your family belonging is yours. On a larger scale, that difference is evident in my national identity being mine and not that of someone from another country. We all, therefore, look at life through our different belongings, with varying interests and points of reference influencing our way of seeing and living life.

Despite this and even because of it, my observation remains that the need to belong is deeply rooted in any individual. It can also be a shared experience, no matter who or where we are. That belonging can embrace neighbours next door, as well as people in one's street, in our hometown, in our nation and indeed in every community in every place, almost without limit, around our world.

My experience is also that such an all-embracing sense of almost total belonging can be consciously enabled, belonging by belonging. That process can be as a result of comparatively small ways by people using their skills and capabilities. For me, they are in designing places.

Crucially, I have also concluded that such belonging can be part of a quite amazing solution to the tragic and all-consuming predicament we are all facing. As a result, there are four key summary themes that I will seek to affirm through the pages in the Steps that will follow. They are that:

a. Success, for me, is in enabling a sense of belonging and that:

b. That enabling is possible by design. I will then even go further and be specific, when exploring my view that:

c. Belonging is directly relevant to how we should respond to the deadly serious predicament we all face. So much so, that crucially:

d. That belonging is then a window to the answer to the deepest of questions anyone can raise, especially those that have within them the positive word, 'why?'

Indeed, I have concluded that belonging is the key to understanding why life on Earth is as it is, even when seen in the context of death. It is also key not only to understanding, but also accessing the originating source of life. For, as you have glimpsed, I have come to see that that source is far more than 'a life essence'.

When glimpsing what lies ahead, I trust you are as intrigued as I was as my life's journey continues. If you are, the Step that follows is entitled:

GOING DEEPER and REACHING HIGHER

A SUMMARY OF QUESTIONS RAISED

All of the questions will be answered as we journey forward Step by Step

Heading One: INTRODUCTION

- Life: what on Earth is it all about?

Heading Two: THE VIEWS OF OTHERS

- If life is in the context of death, what on Earth is life all about?

Heading Three: SCENE SETTING

- Why does Ray Hall think he has something to contribute?
- Why am I highlighting these seemingly obvious consistencies so early on our journey?
- Why are these finite contexts and constraints so immovably there?
- Why is life only able to be lived in the context of finite people, places and time?
- Why does our context in birth have the inevitability of an end in death?
- Why is life not just constrained but full of seeming extremes, with so many in-betweens?
- Why do I and we all prefer the 'ups' and not the 'downs'?
- Why do we, seemingly inevitably, experience both?
- What is belonging?
- Why is belonging so important in all our lives?
- What is the dynamic of belonging in the day to day lives of people and places?
- How can I then enable a sense of belonging when designing places?

Heading Four: A BOY BECAME A MAN

- Why do broken relationships lead to pain?
- Why is pain so painful?

- A child to a young man, but why is the 'me' inside intrinsically the same?
- Was that same 'me' also there as a seed in my mother's womb?
- At whatever age, why am I consistently me?
- Why am I not someone else?
- Why is it that other people are themselves and not me?
- Why can all grow and change in so many ways, but nevertheless remain who we are?
- Why, therefore, am I an individual and as uniquely me as you are you?
- Have others asked those questions?
- Have people in every generation sought answers, when simply noting the way life is?
- Have the questions I am asking here been raised throughout human history?
- Why is it that, generation after generation, we want to know answers to such questions?
- Why is it that relationships can lead to almost blissful happiness, as well as agony when lost?
- Why are relationships so important to the lives of people?
- Why is death seemingly not just in human beings, but also in every dimension of life?
- Why is it that, in life, death always seems to win?
- Why do so many languages exist and not just one?
- Why are there so many different languages, set in the context of a CHALLENGE facing us all and the need to debate by communicating as perhaps never before?
- Why do we want to express identity and belonging?
- Why are there different languages, in the context of our deep need to belong, especially in the context of adversity?

Heading Five: BELONGING AND CONTEXT

- Why can bird fly off a cliff and we cannot?
- What was the brief for our Earth?
- What was life's reason why?
- How should we use every moment, whilst there is time?
- If that is what is needed for a building to be constructed, what is the 'it did not just happen' context for the whole of life?
- We are all then privileged to be able to live out the same pre-planning,

seed of ideas sowing principle in everything we do. What on Earth is going on here?

- Is the definition of 'good', 'bad', 'success' and 'failure' only about adding more time or not to our lives and that of our planetary home or is there something more?
- What is the definition of success?
- What is failure?
- Why is there success and why is there failure in life?
- What is the reference point for knowing what is positive and what is negative?
- Why does success tend to feel good and failure the opposite, namely, bad?
- What is 'good' and what is 'bad'?

Heading Six: A DESIGN BRIEF AND CLOTHING

- A context and a brief must have existed before life existed. But how could that be known?
- Why was opening a door to new insights tantalising?
- If the design of a place is clothing on people, is life itself also clothing on whatever might be that originating something more?
- What if the clothing that is life does not fit the wearer?
- What if the wearer does not realise the clothing does not fit?
- What if the wearer does not know why the clothing does not fit?
- What if the wearer realises his or her attitude to the clothing must change?
- Is the lack of people and place belonging leading to the demise of people and place life here on our Earth?
- Does that world view fit life's many wearers in practice?
- If that world view clothing is leading to negatives, is the time right to consider changing that world view?
- Are alterations only needed, or should a far more radical solution be considered?
- If so, perhaps the time is right to consider a different approach that could mean starting again?
- Had the scheme enabled a sense of belonging and, if it had, was it still doing so?
- Why is it that none of us is, as some have called it, an 'island'?
- Why are we privileged to share in deep relationships within life?

- Why is it that everything we do affects others in some way, ripple by ripple, and potentially on and on, beyond our own limited lifetimes?

Heading Seven: DIAGRAMS

- How many years will I live?
- What is the point of circles, in whatever form, overlapping as one?
- What is the point of caring for and helping others, if my life and all of life is going to die?
- Who can we say, 'Get Jenny' to, if all our equivalents of Kam and Jenny have also collapsed into the same chair?
- Who will we all ask for help?
- How far back does the three-as-one diagram apply?
- How far back has that predicament that we all face been there?
- How can I be certain about anything in life, when it is in the context of death?

Heading Eight: PING PONG BALLS

- How many ping pong balls can touch each other at the same time on a flat surface?
- How many ping pong balls can touch one central ball on a flat surface?
- How many ping pong balls can surround one in 3-D, with each touching the middle ball?
- Why it is that life exists in the form that it does with triangulation here on Earth?
- Why is it that life always seems to be vulnerable to death?
- Why is it that, if the principle of triangulation is not applied to a building, it could become an agent of death?
- Had other students been amazed?
- Had the designers and builders of the Pyramids and the Parthenon learned using their own version of ping pong balls?
- Could the lack of triangulation be a reason why many are now beginning to say that our Earth is in trouble and may soon be uninhabitable, as well as even die?
- Is that then the reason why we are facing a deadly serious predicament?
- Could it also be that we have been denying an intrinsic, even structural rationale in life, so much so that final failure is on the way?
- Could the hidden geometries enable access to a context that might help

me in my intended working life designing places as clothes on the lives of people?

Heading Nine: ALREADY THERE

- Was that already-there design language saying something?
- Was that already-there design language also saying something about the reason why life on our Earth and in our cosmos is as it is?
- If I listened carefully, would I be able to hear what it was saying?
- Could that language reveal the answer to the ultimate question why?
- Could that inherent language hold the key to a world view of theory that outworked in very evidence-based design practice?
- Could its consistency also be key to my goal of enabling a sense of belonging for people in places on a wide range of scales and in an ever-enlarging range of contexts?
- Could that design language enable me to hear and see whatever reason there might be for life being as it is?
- Could it enable me to help others see and hear it as well?
- Could it even help others to know the very reason why life exists?
- Could that language and the reason for life inherent in it then inform every aspect of the way I live and, indeed, the way we all live?
- Could that language even be key to the way we respond to our own inevitable demise, as well as now the deadly serious predicament that has been my point of reference through these pages?
- Could the language of life specifically have as its focus what life is all about?
- Could it also be an expression of that ultimate reason why?
- Could it then enable access to what is 'true' about that reason why?
- Could it even enable an insight into where that 'truth' originates?
- Would I ever know what 'the life essence' was?
- What was that prismatic, life changing experience?
- Am I also saying that each design project can have an equivalent prismatic dimension?

Heading Ten: ALREADY HAPPENING

- How long would it take a SpaceX craft to travel 24 trillion miles?
- What would that climax in history be?

- If that deadly serious prognosis is correct, why did people, especially, in the 19th Century here in the UK get it so wrong in terms of expectations and a world view?
- Have we learned from their mistakes to the degree now needed?
- Why are we now making our global situation worse?
- Is the earlier 'science' about ascendant chaos to order right?
- In the light of current evidence, should the earlier science-based world view be tested afresh?
- Is there something that should then be re-thought?
- Should our Western World and global community get ready for a prismatic change of both world view and thought processes on a scale that would dwarf my own?
- Why do we seem to want enhancement in life?
- Why are some people in such dire situations of poverty that their lives are endangered, whilst others are not?
- Are those extremes also intrinsic in life itself?
- Should we accept them, especially in the context of the global predicament we all now face?
- Should we try to address what some call gross and unacceptable inequality?
- Could that be a component of a much bigger strategic approach to the issues before us?
- Why did earlier generations not stop the environmental damage being inflicted?
- From there, why was it not possible for them to get it right?
- Could this seemingly enormous, almost absolute predicament, have then been avoided?
- Why did serious, let us assume, well-meaning people in the 19th and 20th Centuries think that a utopia was within reach?
- Why, when wanting the best for the people I love, do I find myself contributing toward making our global position worse?
- Am I trapped in something that is unresolvable?
- Are we all, therefore, trapped in a situation that cannot have a positive outcome?
- Is there something wrong, therefore, in every generation, so much so that we cannot stop ourselves making negative contributions to an already dire situation?
- Not just generally, but where specifically in the cosmos can we go?
- I have heard mention of Proxima B in the Goldilocks Zone of the cosmos.

Is it really an option?

- Assuming we can somehow overcome time distance issues, is that a suitable place where life, as we have known it here, could be possible?
- Will everyone alive on planet Earth be able to travel to wherever it is?
- If all cannot travel there, who stays behind?
- Who makes those decisions?
- And how are those decisions made?
- Would I be qualified to make decisions that could affect the well-being of millions of others?
- Did that realisation impact my own life and then my work and life?
- If so, have my thoughts and actions since helped or hindered life on planet Earth?
- How does my focus on enabling a sense of belonging by design affect our shared predicament?
- Are belonging and the proximity of death contradictory?
- Is belonging merely a nice notion that is irrelevant to our dire global situation?
- Is even love for others also irrelevant in the context of that predicament?
- Are the seemingly 'soft' dimensions in life, including a sense of belonging, in opposition to the 'hard' one of terminal decline in our global life support systems?
- Are both belonging and love, therefore, distractions that must be abandoned, so that we can all concentrate on an Earth in trouble?
- If we human beings must leave our dying planetary home, what literally on Earth has life here been all about?
- If I and we have, at least, contributed to the deadly serious predicament here, why do we think we will not do the same in the future, even on a venue in such a wonderfully named Goldilocks Zone?
- Are we all, therefore, in a trap that may be of our own making?
- Are we in a trap that we cannot exit?
- Are we in that trap because the reason for it being there is somehow inherent in what and who we are and, from there, what we do?
- Is the reason for the trap we are all in somehow inherent, not only in what we have done, but in who we are as human beings?

LIFE, WHAT ON EARTH IS IT ALL ABOUT?

IF LIFE IS IN THE CONTEXT OF DEATH, WHAT ON EARTH IS IT ALL ABOUT?

- Do each of my schemes contribute towards fulfilling that answer to the question, even knowing that everything will die?